RUNNING ON ICE

RUNNING ON ICE

THE OVERCOMING FAITH OF VONETTA FLOWERS

Vonetta Flowers

with
W. Terry Whalin

new
hope
PUBLISHERS

Birmingham, Alabama

New Hope® Publishers
P. O. Box 12065
Birmingham, AL 35202-2065
www.newhopepublishers.com

Library of Congress Cataloging-in-Publication Data
Flowers, Vonetta.
Running on ice : the overcoming faith of Vonetta Flowers / Vonetta Flowers, with W. Terry Whalin.
p. cm.
ISBN 1-56309-911-X (hardcover)
1. Flowers, Vonetta. 2. Christian biography-United States.
3. Bobsledders-United States-Biography. 4. Winter Olympic Games
(19th : 2002 : Salt Lake City, Utah) I. Whalin, Terry. II. Title.
BR1725.F519A3 2005
277.3'083'092—dc22
2004026455

ISBN: 1-56309-911-X
N054112 • 0205 • 20M1

DEDICATION

This book is dedicated to
Coach Thomas and the Alabama Striders.

Coach, you and many other coaches dedicate your lives to
helping inner city kids who have little or no hope. But with
your support and encouragement, some of us made good
choices and tried to make you proud by not becoming a
statistic. I share my gold medal and this book with you.

Thanks for believing in me. We did it!

TABLE OF CONTENTS

ACKNOWLEDGMENTS

Jill Bakken—You are the best teammate ever! I owe you so much for helping me realize my Olympic dream. I appreciate you for having confidence in me and our ability as a team. The year 2002 was a very challenging and rewarding year for both of us. I hope you enjoyed the ride as much as I did. I wish you continued success, and a chocolate fountain filled with strawberries.

Bonny Warner—There are only a few people who have changed my life just by my meeting them. There are only a few people who have made me question my faith. And there is only one person who had enough faith in a girl from Alabama to give her a shot at a winter sport. Bonny, that person is you. You deserve so much credit for recruiting some of the best female athletes for the USBSF. Because of you, I was introduced to a new sport, allowed to pursue my dream, and eventually had a chance to represent my country in the Olympics. Although our paths didn't take us to the same destination, I feel that both of us grew because of the time we spent together and the time we spent apart. I wish you all the best and I hope that you, Tony, and Katy enjoy your log cabin.

To all my coaches—elementary school, middle school, high school, summer, and college coaches: Mrs. Ford, Mrs. Young, Mrs. Varner, Coach James, Coach Drake, Coach Clisby, Rod Tiffin, Scott Strand, Coach Phil, Brad Bowman, and Coach Ray—One objective of a coach is to help his or her athletes maximize their physical abilities, develop talent, and direct them on a path that will help them become successful. So why is it that none of you saw my potential as a bobsledder? Thanks for all of the time and energy you put into helping me get to the next level.

The Bobsled Coaches (Bill, Tuffy, John and Tom)—I think all of you realized my passion for bobsled and understood how hard it was for me to almost let my chance to compete for the U.S. slip away. Thanks for what you did to help me realize my dream. I hope to return the favor by recruiting the next great bobsled athlete for you. I'll make sure she's from Alabama!

Jay and Diane Maynard—Words cannot express how grateful I am for everything that you've done. After meeting you, I realized how genuine you were and how generous you were with everything that you had. You made me feel welcome and made me feel like I was part of your family. I will always cherish the time we shared and the many memories of sitting around the fireplace. When I finish with bobsled, I promise to return to SLC so you can teach me how to ski.

Jim and Viv Tidd, Ron and Susan Lockhart, Joan and Sven Kristoffersen, Ron and Marcy Allen, Joe and Carol Dalton, Yvette and Harvey Kaplan, and Anita Price—Thanks for opening your doors, your refrigerators, and your lives to me and my family. I enjoyed getting to know all of you. I'm sure I'll see you soon.

Pastor Mike and the entire Faith Chapel Christian Center family—Thanks for the many prayers and all the ways that you have supported us. Pastor Mike, thanks for providing practical, Bible-based messages. I've learned a lot about who I am and who I'm supposed to be because of your teachings. Your series about "Fear or Faith" has literally changed my life. I wish that everyone could have a chance to listen to this series. The message helped me through some difficult times in my life and gave me peace and confidence during the Olympics and in life. I pray that you and Mrs. Pete will continue the mission that God has for your life

To all my family and friends (and to anyone I forgot to mention)—Most of you laughed when I told you that I tried out for the bobsled team and some of you are still laughing...and though most of you still know very little about the sport, you've supported me in my quest to qualify for the Olympics. Thank YOU!!!

To my mom and dad—Thanks for giving your only daughter the opportunity to travel around the world at an early age. Dad, even though you did not attend a lot of my meets, I knew that you cared and supported my efforts. Mom, as soon as I walked through the door I could always count on you to ask, "Did y'all win?" I'm happy that you were there to watch the biggest victory in my life and there was no doubt that we won...yes, Mom, we did it! WE WON! I love you.

UAB Athletic Department—Thanks for the many years that you supported me. You've been there from my more conventional days as a track-and-field athlete to my more adventurous days as bobsledder. Without your flexibility and support, none of this would have been possible. I'm happy that I had a chance to be part of a young program that is developing into one of the best athletic programs in the state. GO BLAZERS!

UAB Sports Medicine, Dr. Garth, Drew Ferguson, and the entire Sports Medicine Department—Before I even needed medical services, you were there for me and others in my community, volunteering your services, expertise, and time. Dr. Garth, you've never looked for praise for what you do, but you deserve a lot of credit for getting me back on track. Drew, thanks for all you've done and for taking special care of me while at UAB and beyond. As much as I appreciate everyone at UAB Sports Medicine, I hope that I don't have to see any of you anytime soon.

Ross O'Brien—Thanks to you, Ty, and Robert for launching www.vonettaflowers.com. Thanks for your time, knowledge and creativity.

Ty Williams—You've been a great friend for many years and have helped us in so many ways. You and your family are always welcome in our home…just make sure "Tish" brings the chocolate cake.

General Motors—Before I became an Olympian, you supported me and several others through a great program called "Team Behind the Team." This program helped me fulfill a life-long dream and relieved a huge financial burden. I will never forget the day when you surprised me with a brand new car. Our car had over 200,000 miles on it, it had several mechanical problems, and the air conditioning was broken. Not having AC in Alabama during the summers is probably worse than not having heat in Alaska in the wintertime! Thanks for your generous support and for putting me on the road to success.

Power House Gym in Pelham—Ron, you have the best gym in Birmingham! Thanks for working with my crazy training schedule. Working out at 11:00 P.M. or 4:00 A.M. has its advantages. Thanks!

Eskridge and White Physiotherapy—If there was a bobsled trivia question on Jeopardy, I fear that all of you would know the answer. I've shared many of my personal stories as you iced, steamed, and massaged my body back to health. Ethan, I hope that I'll have a chance to watch you compete. I'd love to see you defend your title against the 12-year-olds in your Karate class. Kandi and Mike, don't let Ethan practice his moves on you.

Schaeffer Eye Center—Life is something of a blur when riding down a track at 80 miles per hour. But thankfully, I can see clearly because of your advanced technology in Lasik surgery. Dr. Schaeffer, you and your staff have been a pleasure to work with and have undoubtedly changed the way I see the world.

Shades Valley Rotary—You were one of the few groups that allowed me to talk to you about bobsled in August when the rest of Alabama was talking about football. Thanks for the lunch, the opportunity to meet some great people, and for the honorary Rotarian membership. Your support was very much appreciated.

LPL Financial Services—Dave and Louise Butterfield, thanks for supporting women's bobsled prior to the 2002 Olympics. Corporate support is vital to the success of our team, and your financial gifts helped us with travel, hotels, and equipment. I appreciated the opportunity to meet many of the wonderful people that work for your company.

Barton and Clay Fine Jewelry—Sperry, my wedding rings are a constant reminder of the commitment that I made more than 5 years ago. And the style and beauty is a sign of the commitment you've made to produce fine jewelry. Thanks for all you've done throughout the years. Make sure you plan your ski trip in Torino, Italy, in 2006.

AIT Worldwide Logistics—Thanks for adopting me into your family. And thanks for supporting the USBSF and their athletes.

John Montgomery—You and your staff have been a tremendous help to me and my family. I know I'll never be able to repay you for your kindness, but I hope you know I appreciate all you have done for me. With your vision, I know that Big Communications will continue to grow and develop.

Blue Cross and Blue Shield of Alabama—Thanks for all the support you've shown Johnny and me through the years. Your flexibility enabled me to have my coach/husband accompany me. Your support aided me in my quest. And the managers and associates in Provider Data worked hard to ensure the area continued to exceed its goals. We couldn't have done it without your support.

Laurie Stroud—As a mother, I'm sure you can relate to the balancing act that's involved with nurturing a family and chasing a dream. Thanks for suggesting that I slow down long enough to write this book. It's been a great opportunity. I wish you and Jeff continued success.

To all my family, friends, colleagues, and supporters—Thank you so much! You mean the world to me. And the story goes on....

Foreword by Jackie Joyner-Kersee
ANOTHER OLYMPIAN SHARES HER FAITH

I believe that no one sets out to be a hero or a role model. I didn't. I was simply determined to be the best. I trained hard and worked hard and put everything I had into my competition. One day I had the privilege of standing on the Olympic podium with a gold medal around my neck, singing our national anthem. In fact, I've had that privilege several times during my track-and-field career.

I first met Vonetta Flowers when we were track-and-field competitors in the long jump. We were both in Sacramento, California, for the 2000 U.S. Olympic team trials. It was my fourth and final try to make the Olympic team in the long jump event. The crowds were large and there was quite a bit of media attention around the competition between me and Marion Jones, who placed first in this event. I didn't qualify for the Olympic team, and I retired from track-and-field competition. At this same event, Vonetta also made her last attempt to make the Olympic track-and-field team.

As I think about Vonetta's story, her transition into the women's bobsled competition, I admire her strength. I've seen a quality of toughness in people from Birmingham, Alabama. She didn't put herself into a box, saying, "I can only do track and field." Instead, she entered a completely different sport and it allowed her to perform a feat of greatness.

Vonetta believed the impossible is possible. Every athlete

wants to compete, but changing sports creates a real risk. You don't know what will happen. Vonetta is remarkable—she took the challenge of running in a cold climate and learning about the bobsled, and she was able to take the gold medal and be a winner.

When Vonetta Flowers won the gold medal, I believe it was something God enabled her to do. No one expected much from the United States' second-ranked women's bobsled team; they went into the Winter Games as the underdogs. But Vonetta and her partner, Jill Bakken, knew how to focus and were committed to their goal. They were incredible, and we witnessed Olympic history in their achievement when she became the first African American to win a gold medal in the Winter Olympics.

Recently Vonetta told me the story of how I had inspired her as a young athlete. Twenty-one years ago, Coach Dewitt Thomas planted the seed of the Olympic dream in Vonetta when she was nine years old. He told her, "You have the talent and ability to be like Jackie Joyner-Kersee." This little girl had never heard my name or known anything about my accomplishments until she heard it from her coach. I'm proud that I served as a role model for Vonetta.

INSPIRATION FROM OTHERS

As a youngster, I also drew inspiration from the stories of others. Athletics gave me all kinds of great opportunities in life. But what I'm giving back is far more important to me: I'm showing kids that with determination and courage, they can be successful. I want them to get on the right track with school and their relationship with God. I want to cheer them on—to show them there's so much more to life than winning. That's what some of my role models, such as Wilma Rudolph and Evelyn Ashford, did for me.

Even though I was born in 1960, two years after Wilma Rudolph became the first African American woman to win three Olympic gold medals, her story still compels me to do my best. Although she wasn't accepted in some parts of the United States, including her home state of Tennessee, she didn't let prejudice stop her. The day I got to meet her was like a dream come true.

Remarkably, Wilma traveled around the world and was embraced internationally—yet when she returned home, she couldn't sit at a counter and eat in some places because she was a woman of color. In the later days of her life, Wilma became a mentor and a close friend to me. It was amazing to me that someone of her stature would spend time with me. She taught me some key insights for the journey I would be taking in the days ahead.

Evelyn Ashford was a great sprinter from my alma mater, UCLA. She competed in the Olympics four times, winning four gold medals and one silver. She served as another one of my role models.

AN ATHLETE AND A BELIEVER

Like Vonetta Flowers, I'm a Christian and I can't separate my faith from who I am. If I'm being true to who I am as a child of God, people will gravitate toward me. They'll know I'm a Christian from the way I act. I don't change like a chameleon for different environments, depending on whom I'm talking to. My faith doesn't waver. I've gained a lot of material things from athletics, but that's not what matters long-term. It's my soul, my character, and the God I stand for that mean more to me than anything in the world. I hope everyone I interact with sees that.

Although I do share my faith with audiences, I realize actions speak louder than words. If you don't do things the world does—such as become jealous, insecure, and so on—you aren't controlled by the world. You're allowing God to control what you say and do. Then those distractions and obstacles the devil puts in your path to test your faith aren't so overwhelming. I believe what Scripture says in Matthew 17:20— "For truly I say to you, if you have faith as a mustard seed, you shall say to this mountain, 'Move from here to there,' and it shall move; and nothing shall be impossible to you" (NASB).

Being able to look at the work and accomplish the goal takes a particular mind-set. I meet many young girls who don't know anything about me except what they have read in books. It gives me a good feeling to know that my life has inspired others to achieve this type of greatness.

Now a new generation can be inspired by Vonetta's story through her book, *Running on Ice*. From an early age, Vonetta clung to the dream of Olympic greatness and worked hard day in and day out to train and compete. As you read Vonetta's story, I hope you will be inspired to follow your own dreams and achieve what only God and a life of faith can give you.

CRUSHED DREAMS

In the same month when my Olympic aspirations had been crushed, I found myself moving hopefully down an entirely new path towards my dream, all because of a husband who wouldn't give up and a God who gives us all second chances.

One
CRUSHED DREAMS

As I stepped off the plane in Sacramento, California, I felt the excitement in the air. I was in California to make my last attempt at a spot on the U.S. Olympic track-and-field team. The airport was filled with banners and signs welcoming athletes and spectators to the July 2000 Olympic trials. As I walked to the baggage claim area, I saw athletes I had competed against, some old friends, and some new faces of those eager to compete. It was like a track-and-field family reunion. Even though athletes came from across the U.S., all of us had the same goal in mind—a trip to the 2000 Sydney Games and a chance to represent the U.S. in the biggest sporting competition in the world. For me, it would mean the achievement of a life-long goal.

When I arrived, I had a busy schedule ahead of me. I was there as an athlete, a coach, and a wife. Of course I wanted to qualify for my first Olympic team in the long jump; I was also coaching Nikki Jackson, a student athlete from the University of Alabama at Birmingham (UAB) who hoped to qualify in the 110-meter hurdles. After the competition, my husband Johnny and I planned on doing some sightseeing. Johnny often planned his vacations around my competitions. This trip meant that he would have the chance to visit California for the first time. He had spent hours on the Internet locating the most popular tourist attractions, and had totally planned the second part of our trip. I think he was as excited about seeing Fisherman's Wharf, the Golden Gate Bridge, and Alcatraz as he was about my competition. In any case, I was happy to have him there supporting me.

Johnny and I met on the track team our freshman year at the University of Alabama at Birmingham. We were college sweethearts and dated for six years before we were married on September 25, 1999. We managed to survive some tough growing pains during our college days. At the time of the 2000 Olympic trials, Johnny was working at Blue Cross and Blue Shield of Alabama and I was an assistant coach at our alma mater, UAB. Marrying an athlete was an advantage for me. Because of Johnny's experience as a college athlete, he understood what it took to train and compete, and he also understood the significance of devoting so much time to achieving my goal. Therefore, we were in full agreement when we decided to delay starting our family until after I qualified for the Olympic team. Johnny and I wanted to have six kids eventually, but we agreed that I would take this one last shot at my Olympic dream before we settled down to have kids. I was 26 years old.

I competed in the 1996 Olympic trials in Atlanta, Georgia, but didn't make the team. My husband Johnny coached me in the long jump and the 100-meter race. By the time the 2000 Olympic trials rolled around, I decided to return to my former college coach, Rod Tiffin. Rod was working at the University of Alabama in Tuscaloosa, which is about an hour from Birmingham. I drove to Tuscaloosa in the mornings to train with Rod and then drove back to Birmingham in the afternoons to train my athletes at UAB. I maintained this tough schedule five days a week because I felt it was worth it. I was totally comfortable with Rod's coaching style and confident that he could help me achieve my childhood dream.

A CHILDHOOD DREAM

When I was nine years old I began dreaming about the Olympics. There was not a day that went by that I didn't think about representing my country in the greatest sporting competition of all. While my classmates were deciding what they wanted to be when they grew up, I already knew what my destiny was. I was either going to be an Olympic champion—or a disc jockey! When I wasn't training or competing, I loved to pretend that I was a DJ. I would call into a radio station, disguise my voice so I could pretend to be different people, make requests, and counsel listeners. I had it all planned out…I was going to be an athlete by day and DJ at night. Fortunately, I chose to focus more on running than spinning records.

Growing up, I competed in many track events—always with the Olympics firmly in my mind—during my high school years in Birmingham and college years at UAB. While many track-and-field athletes specialize in one event, I participated in multiple events during each meet, including the 100 meters, 200 meters, triple jump, long jump, hurdles, and the relays. I was UAB's first and only seven-time NCAA All-American in track and field, I had been ranked in the top 10 in the U.S. several times, and I also won a gold medal in the 1994 Olympic Festival in long jump. But none of this was remotely important to me if I didn't qualify for the Olympic team.

In the years after college, while I worked as an assistant track coach for UAB, I continued my own training. I devoted countless hours to lifting weights, eating right, and staying mentally tough. I knew that my time as an athlete was coming to an end, and I'd hoped that the 2000 Olympic trials would prove to be my year to finally find out what it's like to be an Olympian.

However, after all this preparation, my chances of making the Olympic team were put in question. In January of 2000, I hurt my right ankle while training for the long jump, and I had to have surgery on it. I was told the recovery time was four weeks—but that actually meant three or four weeks on crutches, then four weeks of walking carefully on it, then slowly returning to a workout routine. It threw off my regular training and competition schedule. Because of the surgery, I wasn't in peak condition when I went to Sacramento. I knew that it would be very hard to make the team. But I also knew from my years in track and field that all I needed was one good jump to qualify for the finals. Once I made the finals, then I hoped that I would have enough adrenaline left to exceed my personal best and qualify for the team. Deep in my heart I knew that it would take a small miracle in order for me to make this a reality.

The 2000 Olympic trials stage was set and the athletes, coaches, spectators, and event organizers were ready for the trials to begin. The California sun seemed to have saved its most vicious rays until we arrived, because temperatures felt as if they were soaring over 100 degrees. People in the stands were sweating as they sat on the aluminum bleachers and waited for the games to begin. Meanwhile, I was running around warming up my muscles while trying to stay cool at the same time. You could tell that emotions were high by the look on the other athletes' faces, and it was obvious that all friendships would be placed on hold until the trials were over. There wasn't a lot of "How you doing?" and "What's been going on?"—the off-the-field niceness would resume after we battled with each other in the sand. A few minutes before the first round of competition, I sat on the ground stretching my hamstrings while looking at the crowd, listening to the music, and concentrating on my event. I tried to tune everything out and totally focus on my approach down the runway, followed by my landing squarely on the board, and finally, flying like an eagle.

COMPETING WITH JACKIE JOYNER-KERSEE

A lot of the media attention for the women's long jump was focused on Jackie Joyner-Kersee, who was competing in her sixth and final Olympic trials. Since the time I started in track at age nine, I had admired and followed Jackie's career. Jackie, of course, had found success in numerous Olympic events. My first coach, Dewitt Thomas, told me that I could one day be like her. At that time in my life I didn't know exactly who she was, what she had done, or the sacrifices that she endured in order to become a great female athlete. All I knew was that she must have been good for Coach Thomas to keep talking about her all the time. After a few months of him preaching to me about my potential and my future, I started to believe that I could be the next JJK. I latched on to Coach's advice as my personal goal. Now, in Sacramento, I felt I was prepared to compete with my role model. Jackie had been retired for a few years and no one really knew what she could do except for her husband/coach Bobby Kersee. Even though I had competed against her a couple of times, it was always a little weird being so close to the person I admired as a child. But the day of competition is not the time to ask for an autograph or to ask her to pose for a picture. I knew Jackie held the U.S. Olympic trial record for her 1988 jump of 7.22 meters (23 feet, 08.25 inches).

A lot of the focus was also on Marion Jones. She was clearly favored to win the long jump competition. The media had compared this event to the changing of the guard. While JJK was still a fan favorite, most felt that she would need a stellar performance in order to qualify. Her time off had taken its toll, and now it was time to crown a new queen of track and field. While the talk about favorites swirled around me, I tried to ignore these distractions for the most part. From years of competition, I knew that most of the speculation was simply hype and the best person would win the event.

From the posted list, I could see that I was in the second flight of athletes to compete. Jackie Joyner-Kersee was in the first flight, and Marion Jones was in the second flight with me. Many of the women in the long jump were from a particular team or university, but I competed unattached. The athletes who are "unattached" or "not funded" typically do not have a sponsor and are forced to raise funds to support themselves while training for the Olympics. All of the athletes there were very successful in college, but the unattached athletes had not placed high enough in the big meets to entice corporate sponsors. And even though it helps to have sponsorship, everyone was thinking less about how they got there and more about their three trips down the runway. We were all accepted into this meet because we met the qualification mark, and now everybody was on equal ground. It all came down to how we performed that day.

Before the competition started we had a chance to practice our approach and make final adjustments. I felt that my speed was good, I was hitting my mark, and I believed that I was going to pop a huge jump. I walked over and talked with my coach, he gave me the thumbs up, and I waited for my turn. As I sat there trying to stay loose, all of my thoughts were on my jump. The crowd was cheering for other events that were going on, there was an announcer on the microphone keeping everybody up to speed, and other competitors were running down the track; none of that seemed to faze me. I was in my own little world and all I wanted was to win this competition. So as I sat there with my CD player blasting in my ear, I said a little prayer. I thanked God for the opportunity to be here and I also asked for His blessing on my jumps.

* * * * *

When they called the second flight for our jumps, I waited until my turn, got set, and ran toward my mark and leaped as far as I could. I ran down the runway three times, hoping that my jump would be good enough to qualify me for the finals. Unfortunately, after my third and final jump, I did not have a jump long enough to qualify.

I picked myself up off the ground, brushed the sand off, and sat on the ground thinking about what just happened. My dream of going to the Olympics was over. I wanted to cry. I wanted to go home, but I had to be there to coach Nikki when she competed in a few days. More than anything I wanted to be alone. I wanted to step away from track and field, examine my life, and begin thinking about what I was going to do now that I had failed to reach my goal. I had dreamed about this day over and over again and each time I saw myself making the Olympic team. I felt that I was an exceptional athlete and I deserved to be on the team. As all of these emotions were running through me, I slowly put on my sweats and walked over to the athlete warm-up area. Johnny was standing at the gate waiting for me. I was happy to see him and disappointed all at the same time. Not only had I let myself down, but I felt that I let him down as well.

Marion would eventually win the competition, and Jackie would place sixth, failing to make the Olympic team. It was her last Olympic bid. And I had to deal with reality: I was 26 years old, a wife, and a track-and-field coach. It would be very hard to think of delaying our family four more years in search of my spot on the Olympic team. Therefore, I knew that I'd probably laced up my track spikes for the last time as a summer athlete. And it also meant that the team representing the USA in the 2000 Sydney Games would not include a name from Birmingham, Alabama.

ATHLETE WANTED

Johnny has been my greatest supporter and encourager, as well as my coach and husband. After my failure to make the team, he wanted desperately to encourage me and lift my spirits. He knew that I had rarely experienced the feeling of defeat. I also believe that God was guiding him especially at this point. Just a few days after my competition, Johnny accompanied me to the airport and then to the athlete check-in at the hotel in order to register my athlete, Nikki Jackson, who had qualified for the 110-meter hurdles. While I was helping her through registration, Johnny was standing in the hall waiting for us. He looked at the schedule of events taking place at the track, saw some results from previous events, and finally he ran across a flyer encouraging track-and-field athletes to try out for the bobsled team. A member of the U.S. women's bobsled team, Bonny Warner, was holding tryouts in a nearby city. When I walked into the hallway and saw his face, I knew that something was up. Johnny was all excited about the flyer and couldn't believe that they were actually having tryouts in few days.

The flyer read:

Continue Your Olympic Dream by Trying Out for the Bobsled Team

Ideal candidates should be able to perform the following:

30 meters
60 meters
100 meters
Five Consecutive Hops
Vertical Jump
Shot Put Toss

Please call Bonny at [number] or come to Davidson High School track on [date] for tryouts.

The flyer listed several events that would be held: 30 meters, 60 meters, 100 meters, five hops, vertical jump, and shot put toss. After each item it gave an ideal performance and suggested that if you met those requirements then you would probably be a good candidate for the bobsled team.

I laughed at the idea of trying out for bobsled. Johnny thought it would be a fun way to spend the afternoon. He said, "How many of our friends in Birmingham could say that they actually tried out for the bobsled team?" I knew where he was going with this and I didn't want any part of it. Sure, it sounded fun, but I knew nothing about bobsled. Unfortunately, when Johnny gets his mind set on something, it's pretty hard to convince him otherwise. I married a guy who had dressed up in a taco suit during spirit week, and who believed that rolling a friend's house with toilet paper was a high-school weekend ritual. This was just another adventure for him to add to his list.

My entire life had been spent in Birmingham, Alabama, and my idea of fun had nothing to do with ice or snow. Birmingham might get one or two insignificant snowfalls a year. Snow is so unusual in Birmingham that even a little of it shuts down the entire city and closes the schools. At just the mention of snow or ice, people flock to the stores and stock up on bread, water, and other essentials. I had rarely ridden in a car through snow—much less a bobsled.

Johnny started joking with my coach, Rod, and tried to convince him to try out, but Rod was not interested, so Johnny focused all his attention on me. He insisted that if both of us tried out then we could travel together on the team and become the first husband and wife combination to compete in the

Winter Olympics. I knew nothing about the Winter Games and had barely watched them, except for figure skating. All the other winter sports were foreign to me. But I did remember the movie *Cool Runnings* and how much fun they seemed to have trying out for the team.

The movie is loosely based on the true story of the first Jamaican bobsled team, which competed in the 1988 Winter Olympics. The team was made up of track athletes who hadn't made the Olympic track team, but who decided to apply their running ability to the sport of bobsled. Their coach, played by John Candy, urges a friend to believe in his team, saying, "You should see them. They can run like lightning!" "But can lightning run on ice?" his friend responds.

A New Adventure

The idea of me trying out for the U.S. bobsled team sounded like something out of a Hollywood movie. Johnny was convinced that, based on the criteria on the flyer, we could easily make the team. He was still imagining himself as the highly-tuned, weight-lifting, sit-up crunching athlete that he was several years ago. He forgot that he hadn't competed in more than three years and had taken a more leisurely approach to athletics, which included playing an occasional round of golf and his weekly basketball game with the guys from work. Regardless, he wanted to purchase some track spikes so that he would be ready to compete. I was amazed at his excitement, but since this was the start of our vacation and seeing that we didn't have any plans for this day, I was not going to discourage him from giving it a shot.

The next few hours were spent riding around the city looking for track spikes until we found a pair that Johnny liked. I hadn't seen him that excited over buying shoes in a long time. He kept on talking and talking until I was tired of hearing about it, so I agreed to try out with him. I figured that if I promised to try out then he would quit begging me every few seconds.

Johnny didn't know what to expect from the trials, but he thought it would be an adventure we would remember for a lifetime. I remember arriving at the track 30 minutes ahead of time in order to warm up; we expected to find other athletes there. We had warmed up for 15 minutes before anyone else showed up. The more we warmed up, the more I thought about my disappointing performance and decided that I wasn't going to take part in this competition. The joke was going to be on Johnny, because soon he was going to realize that he would have to go it alone. When Bonny finally arrived, there were eight athletes anxiously anticipating the start. Somehow I failed to mention that I was not participating. I didn't want to mess up Johnny's psyche before the competition. I figured that I would wait until the very last minute and spring it on him.

As the competition began, Johnny was looking pretty good until something strangely familiar happened. He was running full speed in the 100 meters when his hamstring tightened up on him about 60 meters down the track. With pain in his eyes and a slight smile on his face, he said he would not be able to continue taking the test, and encouraged me to do it for the family. It wasn't funny, but for some reason it was hard for me to keep myself from laughing. I knew he wasn't really hurt, but he was injured enough that he couldn't finish the competition. I told him he was too out of shape to try and run the 100 meters all out. I really felt sorry for him, so I agreed to take the test and help him live out his dream.

Three-time luge Olympian Bonny Warner had organized the bobsled tryout. Bonny, who worked as a pilot for United Airlines, was a driver for the U.S. women's bobsled team. She was very experienced in luge and was learning the ropes as a new bobsled driver. While other drivers were using push athletes who were recruited by the United States Bobsled and Skeleton Federation (USBSF), Bonny chose to look at the Olympic trials for athletes who met certain weight, height, speed, and strength criteria. Bonny's luge experience was very important, because luge, bobsled, and skeleton athletes use the same ice tracks. Bonny had become familiar with the tracks during her many years as a luger. The luge athletes hurl themselves down the track feet first on a small sled tucked under their back, while skeleton athletes go down head first. They wear a protective helmet but are exposed to the danger of the high speeds as they hurtle down the track. Luge had been an Olympic sport since 1964 and while the U.S. competed in this event, we had never won a medal in it. Many luge athletes eventually became drivers for the bobsled team because they were intimately acquainted with the various turns and twists on the track—which creates an excellent set of driving skills for a bobsled driver.

THE HISTORY OF U.S. WOMEN'S BOBSLED

Women had participated and competed internationally in bobsledding since 1897. The speeds on the track continued to increase and in 1924, because of the increasing speeds on the track and the potential danger, the international leaders of the sport decided women should not participate in the sport.

Seventy years later, in 1994, the United States Bobsled and Skeleton Federation, the U.S. ruling body for the sport, decided it was time for women to reenter the sport. Placing newspaper ads across the country, the USBSF attracted many applications and selected 16 women to try out, then selected eight talented athletes for the first team. These first athletes came from a diverse sports background including track, basketball, soccer, volleyball, and tae kwon do, but they dedicated themselves to learning the sport of bobsled. Because of the newness of the sport in the U.S., it was not surprising that I knew nothing about bobsled. But even though the team had started from scratch, they competed on a high level on the international racing circuit.

At the Nagano, Japan, Olympics in February 1998, Bonny Warner was working as an NBC commentator for the luge event. There she got a chance to closely check out the bobsled event, since it runs on the same track as the luge. At that time, the Olympics only had men's bobsled competitions. Bonny knew that certain people within Olympic circles were lobbying to add women's bobsled as an Olympic medal event. She became interested in bobsled and began helping in the effort. In October 1999, the International Olympic Committee announced that women's bobsledding would be added to the 2002 Winter Olympic Games as a full medal sport.

Now 38, Bonny Warner was preparing to compete in women's bobsled in 2002. She was unofficially recruiting a brakewoman, or what they called a push athlete, for a sled where she would be the driver. The tryout flyer that Johnny spotted was part of Bonny's effort to recruit the best brakewoman to join her sled.

As Johnny hobbled over to the infield, I began lacing up my spikes and for the first time I tried to imagine what it would be like to make the bobsled team. I was familiar with all the sports in the Summer Games, and even though I had never tried…let's say "pole vaulting," I still had an idea of what to expect. I knew absolutely nothing about bobsled. Therefore, I started asking myself a few questions: Where do you practice? How fast does it go? How much does a sled weigh? How cold is it when they actually compete? How dangerous is it? These were just hypothetical questions that I asked myself because I really didn't want to compete. But in the end I decided to go through with it in order to humor my husband.

THE TRYOUT

Bonny set up the tryout with the official U.S. Bobsled and Skeleton Federation six-item test; the goal was to score above the minimum of 750 points. The majority of these events were common track-and-field events for me. When I saw what the events were, I took a step of faith and joined the testing.

The first item of the test involved a 30-meter sprint. Like track, the athletes couldn't start behind the rear meter and they have one or both balls of their feet on the tip to begin. We ran this test three times and our fastest time of the three attempts was scored.

For the second item, we ran the 60-meter sprint, which had the same basic rules as the 30-meters except we only made two attempts and the best score was counted. For the third event, we ran the 100-meter sprint with only one attempt at this event. It was during the 100-meter sprint that Johnny pulled his hamstring.

For the fourth test, I participated in the vertical jump. The vertical jump is simply the difference between a standing reach and a jumping reach measured in inches. They tested us using a Vertec, which is a jump-measuring device. I was accustomed to this type of jumping from my track-and-field work.

The fifth test involved five consecutive hops and was easy for me because of my longtime competition in a track-and-field event called the triple jump. For the five hops, the tape is laid out along the track to about 25 meters, and the 0 of the tape should be on the front of a "toe line." During the test, the athlete takes five two-legged plyometric hops. We are encouraged to jump quickly and not allowed any shuffle steps. If by mistake you do shuffle, you are allowed a second attempt without penalty, but a second shuffle counts as an attempt and isn't scored. Jumps are measured to the athlete's heel. All of my attempts were recorded, then the longest was scored.

The final item of the six-item test involved the shot put. It was thrown forward from between the legs. Each of us made three rounds of throws and the results were recorded, then the best one was scored.

As I completed each item on the test, I could hear expressions of amazement from others at my scores. I thought my scores seemed pretty normal, since I had participated in multiple track-and-field events throughout my college career. Later Johnny told me that he had seen the required ranges for the various parts of the test. Johnny was confident that my scores would be off the charts.

People were saying things like, "Oh my, you're going to Lake Placid!" And I was wondering, *What's Lake Placid?* At that point I had never heard of Lake Placid, New York, the site of the 1980 Winter Olympics and the city where the USBSF is headquartered. Bonny Warner had a more reserved response after my six-item test. She said, "I have other people to test and I'll be in touch with you."

Johnny and I returned home to Birmingham wondering if my future in the Olympics would be in the most unlikely event—the bobsled. We joked about the possibility and were silently praying, asking God for an open door for me to continue in athletics. A week later, Bonny telephoned and invited me to take the next step in the bobsled testing process—a trip to Oberhof, Germany. She was taking four potential brakewomen to see how we performed while pushing a real bobsled on a start track. I accepted the invitation. In the same month when my Olympic aspirations had been crushed, I found myself moving hopefully down an entirely new path towards my dream, all because of a husband who wouldn't give up and a God who gives us all second chances.

BOBSLED 101

A strong push from a powerful brakewoman can make the hundredths-of-a-second difference it takes to win races.

Two
BOBSLED 101

I boarded the plane in Birmingham, Alabama, feeling both great anticipation and deep sadness. I was very curious to see if I would like bobsledding, but I regretted having to leave Johnny only a week before our one-year anniversary. I said a quick prayer and closed my eyes until the plane touched down in Chicago's O'Hare International Airport. I joined the other women in Chicago for our flight to Germany. Throughout my life I had hardly ever seen snow—and now I was going to the German Alps with Bonny Warner and three other women to learn what bobsled was all about. Three of the four of us had never seen a real bobsled, but we were headed to the push track in Oberhof, Germany.

I wondered why we didn't practice on a track in the U.S. Then I discovered that the U.S. doesn't have an on-ice push track; instead, they have a track designed for a bobsled on wheels. It's very similar, except it is built on a railing system, similar to the rails on railroad tracks. The on-ice track has a thick layer of ice that allows the bobsled's runners (steel blades) to glide across as force is applied to the sled. The start house in Oberhof is a partial track, set up to practice one of the critical elements of bobsled— the start. The brakewoman's most crucial role is in pushing the sled at the start. This very short, 100-meter track is designed to help us get a good sense of what it feels like to hit the sled, jump in, and—most importantly—learn what it is like to run on ice.

I had begun to learn everything I could about bobsledding. Bobsled had three categories: two-man bobsled, four-man bobsled, and two-woman bobsled. Women are not allowed to drive a four-person bobsled for safety reasons, therefore women only participate in the two-person event. Now that women could enter the Olympics in bobsled, Bonny needed a brakewoman for her two-person sled. Each team has two people: a driver and a brakewoman. When the pair begins a run, both of them push the sled. The driver is the first one to jump inside, while the brakewoman continues to push. The brakewoman bears the greatest responsibility for pushing the sled, and the driver has the sole responsibility of navigating the sled down the track. Bonny felt that all she needed was a good start to help her become competitive with the other U.S. teams. She had hoped that by posting flyers at the trials and by searching through newspapers that she would find someone with speed and strength to give her the fastest possible start time. She found two of us at the tryouts in Sacramento, she found one athlete from a newspaper article, and the other had taken time off from medical school to try the sport.

My World Expanded

As I listened to the flight announcements in English and then in German, my world expanded in a new direction. This trip marked my first experience into this unique culture. I had traveled many times with track and field, and each time I knew the language and felt comfortable with my surroundings, but this was totally different. I didn't speak German and I knew that the few words that I had learned while glancing through a book wouldn't get me very far if I were separated from the group. Thankfully, Bonny had traveled and spent some time overseas during her luge days and had picked up the language. One second we'd all be sitting around having a normal conversation, and the next thing we knew she'd be speaking German like she had been living there all of her life. I was impressed. I felt better knowing that if I had any questions, Bonny could translate.

I had never been happier to hear the words, "Flight attendants, prepare for landing." I think that was by far the longest flight I'd ever been on. In Birmingham it was 2:00 A.M., and I would normally be in my bed asleep. But people here were wide awake. The local time was 9:00 A.M., and I was ready for bed. As we walked through the airport, I felt what it was like to be in another country. Never before could I imagine what it must be like for an international to come to the U.S. where the majority of the people don't speak her native language. I felt out of place and scared. It was very strange to hear everyone speaking a different language. Occasionally I'd hear a sound that was familiar coming from American tourists or from people in the military, and immediately I felt a connection. I wanted to stop and talk to them, find out why they were over there, what's it been like, and just hold a conversation with someone who knew how to speak English. Instead I made sure I stayed close to the group and continued to look around me and listen with curiosity…I wished I knew what they were saying!

On our way to the hotel as others were checking out the scenery and taking pictures, I found myself intrigued by the taxis. I couldn't believe that the taxis were produced by Mercedes-Benz. I thought that the taxi drivers in the States would love to be a taxi driver over here. As I gazed out the window, I saw snow in every direction. The snow covered the ground, the mountaintops, and the houses. There were ice patches on the streets and icicles dangling off the limbs of the trees. This was a long way from the 90-degree weather I'd left back in Birmingham.

Once we arrived at the hotel, we checked into our rooms

and began looking around the place that we would call home for the next seven days. When we walked downstairs we were amazed to see a real bobsled! We raced each other to see who would be the first to sit inside it. We were touching it, striking poses, taking pictures, and pretending that we knew how to drive. The sleek blue and white bobsled looked like the body of a racecar. It had a hard plastic-like surface, an aerodynamic shape that had been wind-tunnel tested, and an inside built for rugged men. I didn't know what to expect, but I definitely didn't imagine that the seats would be so hard, or that the driver steered the sled with two D-shaped handles connected to a steering system through a bungee cord and a cable. It seemed like it would have been easier to just add a steering wheel.

The next morning we woke up and had some *brot* (bread), ham, and eggs for breakfast. I tried to pick up a few words each day so that I could at least know how to ask for my favorite foods. I quickly learned *bitte* (please), *danke* (thank you), and *mehr* (more).

After breakfast we went to the push track near our hotel in Oberhof. There we met with John Kaus, a U.S. bobsled team start coach who came to work with us. We were practicing outside at the push track. Some of the push tracks are fully enclosed, but this one was outside. I think they were testing our ability to concentrate while working out in the cold temperatures.

The full bobsled track is approximately 1,500 meters in length (nearly one mile), sloping downhill. Various bobsled courses are scattered in different parts of the world. Each of them has to drop a minimum specified vertical distance, and each features numerous banked curves from top to bottom. Each location is unique and has its own characteristics, with varying technical challenges for the driver to maneuver.

BOBSLED EQUIPMENT

Before we went to the track, Bonny reminded us that we would be outside for about two hours and that we needed to dress as warmly as possible. She didn't have to tell me twice. I was not about to freeze. Bonny wore a one-piece speed suit, which looked like a female mechanic's uniform. We wore long tights and long-sleeved T-shirts. Our clothing was not as warm as a ski suit would have been, but we needed to practice in clothing that provided some warmth while maintaining some range of motion/flexibility as we pushed the sled. I was amazed at how little I focused on the cold during the first session. I think the pressure of wanting to learn the sport and the fact that all eyes were on me when it was my turn to push helped keep me warm. It was amazing that my mind was able to block out those frigid temperatures. But as soon as the session was over I was ready to go inside.

Our bobsled spikes are lightweight and from the front and the side they look just like my track shoes, but underneath there is a huge difference. My track shoes have roughly 8–10 spikes on the bottom, and the bobsled spikes have 100 tiny, very sharp spikes on the ball of the foot. These spikes enable us to run on ice and provide the traction needed to grip the ice as we push the sled at a top speed. I could see why these shoes were so important and why I'd probably never need them in Alabama. When we weren't pushing, Bonny suggested that we use spike covers (rubber slippers) to protect the spikes. These covers helped keep the spikes from getting dull as well as keeping any snow from accumulating between the spikes. We also wore lightweight racing gloves to protect our hands from blisters, and they also provided some warmth from the steel handles on the sled.

In addition, at times a bobsledder wears an abrasion vest, sometimes called a burn vest. This piece of protective gear is made of padded nylon. If you crash, you want to be protected, and this is the only thing that will keep some of your skin from being left on the track. All new athletes are encouraged to wear them if they are sliding with an inexperienced driver.

Finally we were given a motorcycle helmet. I laughed when I first saw it. I remembered from the movie *Cool Runnings* that they wore protective headgear, but I figured that it was a helmet made especially for bobsled. I knew that I would have to get used to running with limited vision and added weight on my head, but that wasn't my biggest concern. I kept wondering how my hair was going to look once I took the helmet off. A driver's helmet usually has a clear plastic shield that can swing down to cover the face and protect it from the high-velocity winds during the run. Most brakewomen take their shields off since their faces are down during the run. Having the shield off also helps you feel less trapped and makes it easier to breathe.

It was a far cry from the outfits I had worn in my track-and-field competitions. My life as a track athlete was simple and uncomplicated. The clothing was basic and the shoes standard issue. From my early competitions, we lined up for a race and the best person won. If I had the longest jump, then I won the contest and advanced through the competition.

In contrast, I was beginning to see that bobsled competition for the athlete was much more complex. The variables for the race were much more diverse. The training was completely different, and the equipment was more extensive. I felt intrigued by the sport and felt that I could learn what it took to be successful if I could withstand the cold.

Throughout our time in Germany, we focused only on the start. The start is a 50-meter stretch measured from the starting block and the first set of electric timing eyes. This start area includes a frozen base, plus two grooves in the ice base in front of the block to give the sled runners a guide path to start. When the athletes and sled have broken the light beam between the timing eyes, then the race clock is automatically activated.

We were fortunate enough to have a good relationship with the German team, as they allowed us to use their sled during training. John patiently showed us how to grip the handles on the sled and we practiced "hitting" it. Repeatedly we would run at the bobsled, grip it, and push it down the track on the ice. After we practiced our hits on the sled, John and Bonny taught us how to run with the sled. I found this more natural than hitting the sled and this is where I found my advantage over the other athletes.

Running with the sled is important, but loading (jumping in the sled) is also important. The ideal situation is for athletes to jump in once they've reached their top speed and before the sled starts going too fast for them to jump in. Therefore, the distance for each person is different based on their strength and speed. Because of my experience in the triple jump and the long jump, I didn't find it much of a challenge to jump into the sled at the right time. Others struggled to find their rhythm in this process.

After a few days of practicing two times a day, I really began to feel the jetlag. I wasn't sleeping at night and my body wasn't easily adjusting to the eight-hour time change. We spent about two hours during each session. Each of us took several practice runs during the training sessions. For the first three days, we were learning how to push and perfecting our technique with the bobsled. For the final couple of days, Bonny began to time our starts on the track. Four women went to Germany, but only three of us would be invited to come to Park City, Utah, to see a real bobsled track.

I was not used to the cold weather. I had competed before in the winter, but my exposure to the elements was always limited. Limited exposure wasn't possible when working with the bobsled. Like it or not, you were in the elements for lengthy periods of time. Often I felt frozen, but I said little. I was determined to give the bobsled my best effort and explore whether this opportunity was my way to get to the Olympics.

MISSING JOHNNY

Johnny and I had only been married for 355 days and roughly 12½ hours. I knew because I was marking off the days on my calendar, counting down the hours till our one-year anniversary. We were used to talking to each other about everything, and suddenly we were separated by an ocean of water, time, and distance. Fortunately I had purchased a few calling cards before I left, so each afternoon I'd call home and talk to Johnny about everything that was going on. When we were on the phone it didn't feel like we were thousands of miles away from each other. It felt like our college days when we would spend hours and hours on the phone. Sometimes there was a long silence and other times we would laugh and talk about our time together and why I was over here living out his dream. The calling cards were a great blessing because they gave me a way to connect with Johnny and discuss every detail of the experience, and our conversations also kept me up with his life and the events at his workplace. All of the conversations ended with how much I loved him and how I couldn't wait to see him again.

I felt lonely and isolated during the times between the brief training sessions. Because I had little to do in terms of activity, I spent as much free time as I could on the phone with Johnny. After returning from Germany, I learned that we had racked up a $500 phone bill. I figured that it would be high, but this was outrageous. I called the phone company to make sure that the conversion rate was correct, and they assured me that all of the charges were accurate. This was quite expensive, but my connection to Johnny and the ability to process the different training events with him was a tremendous help to me. It helped me tolerate the loneliness of being away from him.

While we were in Germany, we didn't have much time to do sightseeing. Each day consisted of training in the morning, having lunch, taking a nap, and training in the afternoon. It was kind of nice to be able to look out the window and see the ground covered in snow, but I'd hoped that we would have a little time to do some shopping. I wasn't that fond of standing in the snow, but I could definitely tolerate it long enough to go in and out of the local shops. I was curious to see what was in style in Germany, and I desperately needed to buy something while I was here. All in all I enjoyed watching it snow; it reminded me of what Christmas looks like on TV. As a child growing up in the South, I rarely had a chance to play in the snow, have snowball fights, or go sledding. The only time I ever remember it snowing like this was in March of 1993, when I was a sophomore in college. Birmingham, which rarely gets snow, looked like a winter wonderland. This was nice to look at, but I couldn't imagine living here.

Shannon Hartnett, another of the new girls, suggested that we go outside and try out the sleds that were sitting out back of the hotel. I figured hey, why not? This Californian was always up for something fun. You could see it instantly from the colored streak in the middle of her blonde hair. On different whims, Shannon changed the streak from green to blue to pink. She also sported a funky array of piercings. A six-time women's world champion in the Highland Games, Shannon was strong—she competed in events where women toss telephone poles. I found Shannon's stories entertaining; she knew how to put anyone at ease. At the age of 35, Shannon was a nationally-ranked bodybuilder. She loved the snow and couldn't believe that I had never been sledding during my childhood. Shannon was determined to teach me the ropes.

We borrowed some sleds from the hotel, but these were not your ordinary sleds. These sleds belonged to the kids whose parents owned the hotel. So not only was I about to ride down a snow hill for the first time, I was crazy enough to do it on a sled built for a 10-year-old. "Vonetta, here's how you do it," Shannon showed me. "You sit on the sled and steer with your feet." I jumped on the sled and tried it a few times. While it was cold in the snow, I enjoyed feeling the wind flying past my face as I shot down the slope. The path for our sled went right down a hill and across a small neighborhood road. We had to watch for cars each time we took off from the top of the hill. It was great fun and gave us some outside activities in between training sessions.

Each mealtime was an adventure for me during this trip. I couldn't pronounce the names of most of the foods on the menu. Even though they were translated in English, I still didn't recognize the names of the food. The only two items that I recognized were chicken nuggets and fish sticks. Therefore, I found myself ordering the same thing at lunch and dinner day after day. Often in new situations my appetite disappears anyway, but I tried to eat a bit of food just to keep up my strength for the training and workouts.

During the meals, Bonny told us stories about the luge and the Olympics. These conversations fueled our dreams for the Olympics and the gold medal. She would often punctuate sentences with phrases like, "We're going to win the gold medal." Or "When we win the gold in women's bobsled…." Her goal was firmly in her mind throughout this testing and training period. To everyone around her it was obvious that Bonny had a singular focus—winning the gold medal in the women's bobsled. It accounted for the vast amounts of personal energy she was pouring into the process of finding the best brakewoman for her sled.

While I was absorbing everything I could about bobsled from Bonny and John, my own Olympic dreams were beginning to rekindle. From my days in elementary school, I had clung to the idea of going to the Olympic Games. Every day I worked out and kept focused on this long-term goal. At the Olympic trials in Sacramento when I failed to make the team, it looked like my dreams were ending. Now the dream was getting some new fuel and beginning to revive.

Inside I was quietly praying and continuing to ask God, "Is bobsled my new path to the Olympics?" In faith, I determined a new way to continue to walk through this door of opportunity. The future seemed totally uncertain to me. I was unsure if any of Bonny's talk about gold medals would become reality. I rejoiced in the opportunity to learn a new sport and have the chance to possibly represent my country in the Olympic Games. *I'm going to trust You, God, for the answers to my future in bobsled, and I'll continue to train and work out in this sport as long as You want me here. In faith, I give You my future.*

At this point, I had yet to ride down a bobsled track, but from what I was learning about the brakewoman position and the start of the event, it looked like my adventure was waiting to happen.

FOUR-STORY DROP
IN THE DARK

*I love to ride roller coasters. But what would it be like
to go on a ride where there were no cables or ropes?
Where people have lost complete control, turned upside down
at 80 miles per hour, and then flipped off the track?
What would it be like to go on a ride where people have died?*

Three
FOUR-STORY DROP IN THE DARK

I could see the determination in her eyes. Bonny Warner was driven to be on the first women's bobsled team to get to the Olympic Games. Her focus was an example to me and the others as we finished our time at the start track in Germany and returned home. A few days after returning, Bonny called my home and said, "Vonetta, I'm inviting you to come to Park City, Utah, in early October to take your first bobsled ride and see if you even like the sport." Our time in Germany gave me a taste for the work of being on a bobsled team, but I had never ridden down the track. In Oberhof, we trained on a short start track and pushed the bobsled back and forth to practice the initial push for the sled. What would it feel like to ride down the track at 80 miles per hour?

I love to ride roller coasters. I remember as a child standing in line at Six Flags waiting for my turn for a ride on the Scream Machine roller coaster. As people stepped off the ride, some were smiling, some were frightened, and others had tears rolling down their faces from the fierce winds. It seemed a little strange, but everyone in line wanted to be scared to some degree. I was confident in knowing that the ride was tested, firmly secured to the frame, and basically safe for kids of all ages. Therefore, I was willing to take a ride and felt comfortable in the fact that I would return in one piece. But what would it be like to go on a ride where there were no cables or ropes? What would it be like to go on a ride where people have lost complete control, turned upside down at 80 miles per hour, and then flipped off the track? What would it be like to go on a ride where people have died? Everyone I knew who had ridden a bobsled instantly discounted any comparison to a roller coaster. While almost everyone has ridden a roller coaster at some point in their life, few have hurtled down a bobsled track.

I rode to Park City with the sister of Olympic gold medalist Bonnie Blair. Bonny Warner has a good relationship with Bonnie Blair, so she asked her sister to give me a ride. The engine in our car struggled to climb the mountain road up to Olympic Park. After 45 minutes of driving through the mountains, we finally reached snow country. We headed to one of the most popular ski areas in Utah and the chosen site for the upcoming 2002 Winter Olympics. As we pulled through the Utah Olympic Park gateway, someone pointed to the bobsled run. The finish line for the run is at the bottom of the mountain and my eyes traveled higher and higher until I could finally see the top of the run.

In a short time, I learned a lot about the track and about the sport of bobsled. This was one of the world's newest tracks and only the second bobsled track to be built in the U.S. I learned that in the winter months, the track is artificially cooled and a thick layer of ice is formed over the concrete so the bobsled's runners (steel blades) can glide smoothly on the ice. In the summer the track is used for passenger rides—people ride in a bobsled fitted with wheels, which allow it to travel down the course without steering. This track features the fastest speeds of any artificially iced track. Built at a cost of $25 million, the track features 15 curves and is 1,335 meters long (⁸⁄₁₀ of a mile). The vertical drop on the track is 390 feet—like dropping from the top of a four-story building. On the ice, the sleds run an average of 81 miles per hour and can go up to speeds of 90 miles per hour with the average run time of 48 seconds.

I could see the top of the track split into two areas. One side marked the beginning of the men's luge. Luge is the Olympic event where the athlete drives a small sled feet-first down the track; Bonny Warner had been a part of the U.S. Olympic team in this event. The men start in a seated position and use the spikes on their gloves to help them grip the ice in order to generate speed in the start area. After a short distance, the luge track connects with the bobsled/skeleton track.

The bobsled team shared their start area with the skeleton athletes. In the skeleton event, individuals race head first, with their face 6 inches off the ground, their hands gripping the side of the sled as they approach speeds near 80 miles per hour. The athlete takes a running start and then jumps onto a single sled, which races down the same track as the bobsled.

I quickly learned that as bobsled athletes, we had to be in good physical condition. Not only did we have to push a 400-pound sled, but we also had to lift it in and out of the truck before and after our runs. The sled is transported in a diesel double-cab pickup to the start area. We had to hang on in the back hoping that they wouldn't take a curve too fast. We had a red bobsled with the United Airlines logo on the side of it (the sponsor for the team that Bonny Warner was assembling). The blades of the sled fit securely between wooden grooves cut specifically for them. The transports had metal handles, which enabled us to move the sled by picking up all four ends at the same time. The sled is then moved to the staging area at the top of the track. All athletes have to keep their sleds in this area during the race.

In the staging area, there is a small booth with glass windows where, during a race, the officials sit to monitor the progress. Near the start area is a small two-story building called the "start house." Athletes stand inside to keep warm and wait for their chance to compete. There is also an observation area on the second floor that has a fabulous view and is also a great spot to watch the event.

MY FIRST RIDE

It all seemed so surreal. "What am I doing here?" I asked myself. "Do I really want to learn how to bobsled?" I wished that Johnny could have been there with me. He has a way to make difficult situations seem less stressful. In the midst of my daydreaming, Bonny called my name and asked me to help her move the sled to the line. We slowly walked the sled over to the top of the track. We placed the sled on its side and slid it onto the ice. I had no idea what to expect. I was no longer standing in line at the amusement park. This was the real thing. Bonny and I were standing in the bitter cold, and I was preparing to take my first ride down the track. I wasn't worried about our time, my form, or anything else for that matter. My number one priority was getting in the sled.

Bonny and I fastened on our helmets and removed our outer jackets. We tightened our gloves and got in position to push the sled down the track. My pulse was racing as I thought about my first ride down the track. I had not been nervous until we stepped on the ice. I realized that this wasn't anything like the races I had participated in in the past. The finish line wasn't straight in front of me. We had to make several sharp turns, which required good hand/eye coordination. At that point I barely knew Bonny, but for some reason I was fine with placing my life in her hands. I had never seen her race, I had never watched video of her going down this track—for all I knew this could have been her first bobsled run. She was very convincing when she spoke about the Olympics and had motivated me to think that we had a chance to win a gold medal. And that's why I stood there with my Olympic dreams in sight, with my faith in God and in a woman I barely knew.

A few weeks before, Bonny and I had practiced the start in a controlled environment. The track in Germany was not scary at all. I wasn't afraid of the track in Park City. I feared the unknown. Because of the repeated practice sessions, I took a familiar position on the sled to push. I gripped the two handles on the top at the back of the sled. Bonny stood in front of me and gripped the driver handle on the front of the sled. Then I knew it was time. I yelled, "Back set!" Bonny began, "Front set, Ready, Go." In the beginning everything felt comfortable; it was just like we practiced. After a few seconds in the push area, Bonny jumped inside the sled to the driver's seat and grabbed the D-rings and was ready for action.

While Bonny got set to drive the sled down the track, I continued pushing with all my might, hoping to give us a fast start, but focusing on my load, or entry, into the sled. At the right moment, I jumped with both feet into the back of the sled, gripped the handles inside the sled, and tucked my head down between my knees. With every second down the hill, the momentum of the sled increased and we were bound for the first of 15 curves in the track.

The sled was bouncing around on the ice as we drove toward the first curve. For the entire way down the track, I was completely in the dark. The only lights I saw were the four spots in the bottom of the sled where the metal runners connect to the fiberglass body of the bobsled. My neck and head begin to feel the G-force pressure as we headed into the curves.

When a person is standing on the ground, they have a G-1 force of gravity. When the astronauts ride a rocket into space, their gravity weight triples to a G-3 force. On the bobsled, the G-force is somewhere between G-4 and G-5. I could feel the pressure on my chest as we shot around the curves. It was almost like I was socked in the chest, and the force knocked the wind out of me. I learned quickly during this first trip on the bobsled to hold my breath on the curves and suck in a quick breath during any straight portion. I held on for dear life. It felt like we were going to tip over at every turn. I don't think I ever prayed to God so many times in such a short period. I was clenching my teeth, squinting my eyes, and holding onto the metal handles with every ounce of energy.

I could hear the metal runners of the sled bounce across the ice as we barreled down the track. In the middle of this situation, I was supposed to be relaxing. I know it sounds impossible, but as the body's muscles relax, the sled will go faster. I couldn't have relaxed, but it was just as well—I had about all of the speed that I could stand for this ride! Then suddenly I felt Bonny's elbow knocking on my helmet.

Typically after a few rides, the brakewomen learn the track and can tell when they've crossed the finish line. Since this was my first run, Bonny said she would let me know when it was time to brake. I reached between my legs and pulled up on the handle, which caused the metal teeth to scrub along the snow and ice and eventually stop the sled. I was happy that it was over.

Bonny, on the other hand, was pumping her fist and was excited about the drive. I learned that drivers can tell whether they had a "clean"—good—run or not. The good drivers have an idea of what their time is based on how they feel after the race. It was apparent that Bonny knew her time was good. It was her first time in several weeks to drive the sled down a track, and from the look in her eyes I could tell she loved every second of it. I smiled and tried to look at ease about my first ride, but my heart was beating so fast. Inside, my arms and legs felt stabs of new pains from the G-forces.

While I had tried to prepare for my first ride, no one told me about the G-force and the added pressure from the speed around the curves. Now my head was spinning and I felt dizzy. I just wanted to sit down and gather my thoughts. After most rides at an amusement park I want to rush back to the front of the line and do it again, but in this case I was in no hurry to rush back down the track. I wondered if the next trip would be a little better if I just kept my eyes closed the entire time.

I thought, *What have I gotten myself into?* We moved the sled out of the way in the finish area and snapped it back on another set of wooden supports, then lifted it on the back of the diesel pickup truck. As we took off our helmets and jumped into the back of the pickup, the driver started the engine and began to take us back to the start area.

"How was it, Vonetta?" Bonny asked me with expectancy in her eyes. "Are you ready to do it again?"

"Sure," I replied. After I caught my breath, I began to really appreciate the ride. I had fun! I liked the adrenaline rush, the speed, the curves, and the fear that came along with bobsledding. I couldn't believe that I had a chance to participate in something like this in the Olympics. The other athletes were right. The bobsled ride didn't compare to a roller-coaster ride. It was much better!

I will always remember my first ride down the track. There was nothing that anybody could tell me or nothing that I could have done to prepare myself for this awesome ride. From my perspective as the brakewoman, it was truly a four-story drop in the dark.

New Friends

I was amazed at how much I had learned about the sport in just a few months. This was the beginning of hundreds of similar rides down the track. I had a feeling that this was going to be a great opportunity. My goal was to come out to Park City and determine if I liked bobsledding. After a few runs I had fallen in love with this winter sport and was looking forward to spending a lot of time going down this track. But first we had to qualify for the national team.

None of the three women, including myself, whom Bonny invited to come to Park City and train on the bobsled track were a part of the United States bobsled team. Because our status was unofficial, we were training on invitation from Bonny. The Bobsled and Skeleton Federation and the Olympics didn't have any extra funds for our participation. Bonny was an airline pilot, and she knew many other pilots and their families who lived in the Park City area. Because Park City was only 45 minutes from the Salt Lake International Airport and since many airlines used Salt Lake City as one of their hubs, many pilots from different airlines lived in the region.

As I heard the story, several months before I became involved in bobsled, Bonny and the wife of a local pilot organized a picnic on a weekend. Various Park City families were invited to the event and Bonny gave a short talk about the Olympics, sharing her dream of winning a gold medal in women's bobsled and the lack of funding from official sources. "There are many practical ways for you to help me, along with a number of other women, to achieve our dreams," Bonny explained. Then she encouraged people to volunteer on a sign-up sheet for a variety of tasks such as housing the athletes, feeding the athletes, or volunteering to haul sleds and equipment at the bobsled run. Another volunteer position was to run a video camera at the start and the finish of the bobsled run. The tapes were used to monitor the driving and push techniques so the athletes could improve during their training.

The crowd listened to Bonny's inspirational stories, then eagerly signed up for the various possibilities. These pilots and their families had no agenda or motivation other than simply wanting to help some talented young people achieve their

Olympic dreams. Two of the couples at this gathering were Ron and Marcy Allen and Jay and Diane Maynard.

My first week in Park City, I stayed at the home of Ron and Marcy Allen. A pilot for Delta Airlines, Ron and his wife Marcy were traveling when I arrived at their house, and they left Bonny the code to enter their garage door. There was one slight hitch with my sleeping arrangements; throughout my life, my family had always kept a stray dog in the yard by feeding it scraps from the dinner table. I had never stayed with anyone who actually kept a dog in their house until I stayed at Ron and Marcy's house. The Allens kept their large, frisky golden retriever named Butterscotch inside their home. While it was unlikely Butterscotch would hurt me, he bounded toward me and jumped on me every time I entered the house. I barricaded myself in the spare bedroom so I could avoid the dog jumping on me. But in any case, Ron and Marcy were incredibly gracious and kind hosts during my first trip to Park City.

Two weeks later I stayed with Diane and Jay Maynard, who didn't have any pets or children in their house. Their only son, Patrick, lived in California. An American Airlines pilot, Jay Maynard and his wife, Diane, almost adopted me into their family, and I lived with them at various times over the next two years. Shannon Hartnett, the Highland Games World Champion, also lived with the Maynards. Shannon and I could not have been less alike. Shannon was outgoing and full of energy. She was always trying to make me laugh. I discovered that Shannon didn't believe in the United States' Pledge of Allegiance and refused to say it when she was in elementary school. Quite the opposite, I loved the Pledge in elementary school and repeated it often when I didn't have to say it. Even though we were opposite types of personalities, because of our commitment to the sport of bobsled, we became close friends.

Diane and Jay turned over the upper floor of their home to

Shannon and me. I slept in the "peach room" and Shannon slept in the "purple room." We loved Diane and Jay's laid-back personalities, their willingness to accept us into their home and adopt us into their family routines. Normally we would sleep late (until 8:00 or 9:00 A.M.), then get up for a high protein breakfast of eggs, fruit, orange juice, and bacon, plus some of Jay's special pancakes. Then we would head to a local gym to run and lift weights.

Every day our bobsled track time was scheduled from 4:00 P.M. until 8:00 P.M. Since luge and skeleton athletes and other bobsled teams used the track, time on the track was a precious commodity, so when we got some time, we took it and intensely used it. Volunteers like Jay and Ron would help us run the sleds back and forth into the truck and haul it up the hill so we could take as many practice runs as possible down the track. A tremendous amount of energy and effort goes into bobsled practice and training every day. Normally we had one day off during the week for rest, but we did something to prepare every day of the week.

After a hard day of practice, Shannon and I would arrive back at Diane and Jay's house. Often Diane would make some of her special spaghetti and we would load up on the carbohydrates and energy from the pasta and meatballs. The dinner table was filled with animated conversation about our practice session.

After clearing the table, Shannon and I would spend another hour on bobsled stuff. Thankfully, the Maynards have a heated garage, which was a valuable resource in the cold weather of Park City, Utah. The outside temperature often dropped well below freezing before 9:00 P.M, and we still had more work to do on the sled. Jay parked our bobsled inside his garage and we spent time sanding the bobsled's runners. We shared our goals of making the U.S. women's bobsled team and formed a unique relationship.

Shannon and I used sandpaper to work over every single inch of the metal runners' blades. During our practice runs, tiny nicks would begin to appear on the runners. The smallest imperfection can affect the speed and outcome of the run. We sanded these runners to return them to their perfect condition so they would be ready for the next day's workout session.

After Shannon and I finished sanding the blades, we would call it a night and head to our bedrooms for some much-needed rest. One of those nights, as I drifted off to sleep, I reflected on how my athletic career had grown in complexity. For many years, I consistently trained and worked out and practiced my running and jumping in the area of track and field. The continual effort had reaped remarkable results and rewards in terms of my opportunity to travel and compete in many different places around the United States. With each opportunity I thanked God for His blessings in my life and for my athletic ability. Now with women's bobsled, I was learning the dedication and sacrifice it would take to become successful. I trained and practiced and learned about some of the complexities of the sport. Many variables played a key part in the outcome of the event—from the tiniest nick in the blade of a sled runner, to the amount of energy and strength I invested in getting the sled out of the start area, to the steering excellence of the driver, to the condition of the ice on the track. Most races were separated by hundredths of a second. In faith, I was trusting God to open the door for my continued involvement in women's bobsled. As Jesus told His disciples in Matthew 17:20, "I tell you the truth, if you have faith as small as a mustard seed, you can say to this mountain, 'Move from here to there' and it will move. Nothing will be impossible for you."

I felt that I had a small amount of faith regarding the bobsled and the Olympics. While Bonny Warner continually talked with us about the possibility of getting into the Olympics—our goal was clearly within our sights—it would take a tremendous amount of effort and simple faith to make it on the women's bobsled team. In faith, I continued moving ahead and working hard every day to see if this door of opportunity was the one that God would use in my life. Each day marked another step in the journey.

JUMPING DEEPER INTO WOMEN'S BOBSLED

Women's bobsled had reached a new level when it gained Olympic medal status, and there was a great deal of media excitement around the sport. We had hit the big time!

Four
JUMPING DEEPER INTO WOMEN'S BOBSLED

"Vonetta, you want to make sure you lean into the sled like this," John, our start coach, reminded me after another practice run. I was trying to soak it all in. Bonny and I were in Park City, Utah, training during our first season together. Bonny had chosen me to be her brakewoman, or pusher, for her sled and we were training for the regular season of the women's bobsled competition.

I was quickly learning that there was much more to being a great pusher than just being fast. I knew from my brief experience that other great athletes like Herschel Walker, Willie Gault, and Edwin Moses had participated in bobsled. Herschel Walker and Willie Gault were professional football players who had given bobsled a try. Herschel Walker was a well-known Southeastern Conference (SEC) football player who was famous for winning the Heisman Trophy before going on to the NFL. Also, the legendary Edwin Moses, a two-time Olympic gold medalist in the 400-meter hurdles, entered the sport of bobsled after retiring from track and was known as one of the top two or three brakemen in the world. These were exceptional athletes within their sports and based on their strength and speed alone, I didn't understand why they were not successful in bobsled. I was in no way comparing my athletic abilities to theirs, but I was very curious and wanted to learn the proper technique as quickly as possible. I knew that every tenth of a second that we could shave off our push time at the top would theoretically save us up to three tenths of a second at the bottom. My goal was clear and I was focused on becoming the best brakewoman in the world.

NASCAR MAKES A BOBSLED

As I learned about the sport of bobsled, I was aware of the importance of excellent equipment and particularly the sled itself. In the history of the sport, one of the revolutionary changes came in 1992 when Geoffrey Bodine worked with Chassis Dynamics to develop a new bobsled they called the Bo-Dyn sled. After watching the 1992 Winter Olympics, Geoffrey, the NASCAR legend, was intrigued by bobsledding but disappointed in how the U.S. team finished. He began researching the sport and saw some parallels between bobsleds and racecars. He believed that American technology, especially racecar engineering, could be successfully applied to bobsled to help make the U.S. bobsled team more competitive. During the next few weeks he would take a ride down the bobsled track in Lake Placid, New York. Two years later the first Bo-Dyn sled was officially introduced to the world at the 1994 Winter Olympics at Lillehammer.

Over the next few years Geoff Bodine became more excited about bobsled and even began to look at other designs. He studied the German Dresden and decided that he could incorporate some of the technology with the Bo-Dyn. The result of this study became the second generation of the Bo-Dyn sled called the Bo-Dyn II. This type of bobsled combines the best of two technologies—it's a hybrid of the original Bo-Dyn and the German Dresden. The frame and the suspension were modified for this new version. Also, the Bo-Dyn II includes a different push bar design so the teams can load more efficiently and reduce their push-start times. In addition, the rear push bars were raised and the driver's push bar was extended for better leverage. The lower rear seat pan positions the driver and brakeman more aerodynamically in the sled. This new type of sled is 150 pounds lighter than a traditional sled. The reduced weight allowed for a stronger crew to generate more power at the start. As brakewoman, I was not too concerned about the design or the nuts and bolts of how the sled was put together, as long as it was safe. I just wished that they would have added some padding. I had several bruises on my knees from my helmet bobbing back and forth while sliding down the track. But I was fortunate that I had not crashed.

In October 2000, the entire U.S. women's bobsled team began training in Park City on the ice. I moved back in with Jay and Diane Maynard and had to adjust to the G-forces, getting banged around at practice, working out with weights, and being away from home. I began to feel more and more comfortable staying with Jay and Diane. I grew up in a predominantly black community and had very few white friends besides the ones on the track team, and at first I was not sure what to expect. Jay and Diane accepted me into their family, allowed me to stay in their home even when they were out of town, and treated me like their daughter. At first it was hard to believe that people could be this trusting and so nice to a total stranger. But meeting them and the others in the community helped me feel more at home and gave me peace that I don't think I would have had if I had been stuck by myself in a hotel room.

During those first few days of practice I had a chance to meet the other girls on the team and learn more about the people that I would spend the next four months with. There were basically four teams competing for three spots.

Jean Racine and Jen Davidson were USA 1. They had been the most consistent team over the past three years. They were currently ranked #1 in the U.S. and #1 in the world. They were best friends and thought to be the favorites to win the gold in 2002.

Jill Bakken and Shelly Stokes were USA 2. Jill was part of the Army's WCAP (World Class Athlete Program). Shauna Rohbock was Jill's #1 brakewoman and best friend. They joined WCAP together with hopes of representing the Army and their country. Jill was sliding with Shelly because Shauna was out for a few months nursing an injury. Athletes who are part of this program are allowed to participate in sports on a full-time basis while serving their time in the military. Shelly was a 1996 Olympic gold medalist in softball.

Bonny Warner achieved USA 3 ranking from her performance in 2001 with her former brakewoman. Now that we were together, I would also take on the USA 3 status until team trials.

Elena Wise, the fourth driver, was a former brakewoman who had decided to drive and was believed to have the talent to challenge the other teams.

As with any team, it became obvious that some of the girls were closer than others. Bonny was several years older than everyone else on the team and was more focused on making sure that she was not overlooked and that her point was heard. I have always taken the "look and see" approach before making a judgment, so I didn't say much in the beginning. The other girls on the team were trying to feel me out and determine my personality. They would often ask questions like…"What's wrong with your driver? Why is she so uptight?" I just figured that this was her personality and her means of communicating. But based on those comments, it was obvious that they were not going to invite us over after practice to watch a movie or for a game of Scrabble. It would take months before I would have a chance to really get to know the girls on the team and even longer before they would tell me how they really felt about me and Bonny.

As the weeks progressed, I began to listen to comments that Bonny made and started to understand some of the challenges she was facing. Each driver is given a sled and a set of runners based on their ranking. Since Bonny was ranked #3 in the U.S., then she was allotted the third-best sled and the third-best set of runners. Well, Bonny didn't like the number 3. She had achieved most of her goals in her life based on hard work, persistence, and driving herself until she got what she wanted, and bobsled wasn't going to be any different. She wanted the best sled, the best set of runners, and the best brakewoman. Therefore, she teamed up with Pat Powers's Eagles Bobsled Club with hopes she could even the playing field. With his financial support she felt that she could afford the best equipment, training, and coaching beyond what the bobsled federation was offering the team.

I also became a member of Eagles Bobsled Club. Before the season started, Bonny asked if I would sign a contract stating that I would only slide with her. I figured that the other teams were picked and since Bonny chose me to be in her sled, then I had no reason to leave. I signed the agreement, not knowing that Bonny was the only driver who required her brakewomen to sign contracts. In any case, Bonny and I were a team and I believed in her abilities as a driver and hoped that we were headed to the Olympics.

Our first objective in making the Olympic team was to perform well during the team trials in Salt Lake City. This would mark our first race together and it would also give us an idea of where we stood against the other U.S. teams. Based on our times in practice, we felt that we had a good chance to be competitive. Our start times were very good and Bonny's second year of driving was proving to be better than she expected. Jean Racine would eventually win the trials, Jill Bakken placed second, and we came in third. I don't remember much about the race, but I will not forget how I felt when I realized that I was going on tour with the bobsled team. Even though I was working hard and taking daily trips down the track, my purpose and vision was still not clear. All my life I wanted nothing more than a chance to represent my country at the Olympics and now it seemed like it was happening in an unusual manner. My life was taking a drastic turn, and in the back of my mind I wondered, had God led me down this path or had Johnny gotten me into this crazy cold winter sport? For now, all seemed to be going well.

Later that night Jay and Diane surprised me with a birthday cake. I celebrated my 27th birthday with my new family and friends. I was also happily surprised that Johnny was able to come out and watch my first bobsled race. I had been keeping him up to date and getting him prepared for the cold and it felt really good to have him there with me. After ice cream and cake we went over to a dinner sponsored by Eagles Bobsled Club. I will never forget that night because Shannon Hartnett was wearing a waist-length pink fur. I shouldn't have been surprised to know that she had something like that in her wardrobe, but to actually see it on her kept me laughing all night. The dinner was held in honor of our team qualifying for the World Cup tour and it was also used as an etiquette course. Pat supported Bonny's and Todd Hays's team, and apparently some of the guys had not displayed proper etiquette over the past few years while eating in public. I could tell that some of the guys were trying to pay attention while others could care less if you ate with the dinner fork during dinner or with the salad or desert fork. It was a nice way to celebrate our start together and bring the team together before the season began.

We would have roughly two weeks to go home before we left for the first half of the season. I returned to Birmingham to find my bed, which I love dearly, still there, and my plants, which Johnny had killed. I know that he had been busy with his job and was probably sick of eating frozen dinners, so I tried to be understanding. But I know that I must have asked him ten times to water my plants. I tried to bring them back to life, but the brown, withered leaves didn't respond well to water or me talking to them.

The next few days were spent meeting with my girls on the UAB track team and catching up on what had been happening with them while I was away. I really hated leaving my first recruiting class and I know that most of them had signed with UAB because of my experience on the national level. It was very hard to leave them, as I knew that they would not have a shoulder to lean on, to cry on, nor would they have me fussing at them for wearing their clothes too short or too tight. I missed my girls, and part of me wanted to stay and help them achieve their athletic goal. Another part of me realized that I had an opportunity that might never come again, and as much as I wanted to stay, I couldn't let this chance slip away. Thankfully, the university gave me the time and flexibility that I needed to compete.

FIRST SEASON ON THE CIRCUIT

The U.S. women's bobsled team, including me, left for Europe in November 2000. The World Cup races were to take place December 1 and 2 in Winterberg, Germany. I was excited about competing on this level and about getting to know other sliders from around the world. I was also getting more comfortable with this traveling thing, and with living in cold weather.

Women's bobsled had reached a new level when it gained Olympic medal status, and there was a great deal of media excitement around the sport. We had hit the big time! Women athletes from other sports wanted to try their hand at getting a bobsled medal. There were two crucial elements to getting the winning edge in bobsled. One was an explosive start, and the brakewoman is key for this. Athletes frequently come out of track to become brakewomen. I was one of these. The other crucial element is a driver who knows how to get every ounce of speed out of the track and the sled—without crashing, of course. Luge athletes know the track very well. Bonny Warner came to bobsled after being a luge competitor. Two other well-known luge athletes who made the switch to bobsled at the 2000 World Cup competition were Germans Susi-Lisa Erdmann and Sandra Prokoff. Bonny knew them well from her years in luge. Their intimate knowledge of the ice track made them excellent bobsled drivers. We would compete with them often in the next year, and for several years Susi-Lisa, Sandra, and Jean Racine would trade the 1-2-3 spots in World Cup standings.

For me, there were many adjustments in this bobsled schedule. I was learning what it meant to be a full-time athlete in a winter sport. I continued to feel lonely without Johnny at these events and I was also missing the comforts of my home. I wasn't sleeping well and I was eating different foods, but I was determined to continue ahead in this opportunity that the Lord had graciously given me.

The World Cup bobsled events are held at various ice tracks in the world over the course of a season. Two heats are held on one day for each event. The winner of each event is the crew with the lowest combined time. Each trip down the track takes less than a minute, so the combined times are less than two minutes. The top-seeded crews get the best start positions at all the events, and get to go down the ice first, before it is torn up by the sleds. There are two race events in each World Cup location, usually held two days in a row. Bonny had told me how well we could do, that she was a great driver, and I had entered the race hoping we could win.

In race one at Winterberg, our teammate Jean Racine won the top spot with a combined time of 1 minute, 57.38 seconds. German Sandra Prokoff won second and Francoise Burdet of Switzerland took third place. Jill Bakken and Shelly Stokes ended in seventh place, and Bonny and I took ninth, with 1:58.56. The U.S. women's bobsled team had only two Bo-Dyn sleds, and the top two crews used those. Bonny and I were driving one of the older, slower sleds. The Eagles Bobsled Club had ordered a new Bo-Dyn for the women's team, but it wouldn't be delivered until the next summer.

The results of race two at Winterberg almost exactly matched the first—Jean in first, Jill in seventh, and Bonny and I moved up a spot to eighth place. I was kind of disappointed at our performance. The next week at the World Cup races three and four in Igls, Austria, Jill Bakken injured her knee before a race and had to withdraw from the competition. Bonny and I got to use the second Bo-Dyn sled, and we placed sixth in race three. I was beginning to think, *Bonny, this is not what you told me. You said we would do well and that you were a good driver.* Bonny told me, "I'm better on the tracks in the States." She said that she would do better in the second half of the World Cup season, which was in Lake Placid and Park City. In race four at Igls, we took third place with 1:50.77, and I won my first-ever bobsled medal, a bronze. Jean Racine took the gold with 1:50.17—we were less than a second behind her.

I had just completed the first series of races in my introductory season on the women's bobsled circuit. The U.S. team went home for a holiday break. During the first week of January they returned to Park City, Utah, for the U.S. national championships, where the U.S. women competed against each other. According to the U.S. bobsled rules, the driver could select any brakeman for their sled, and Bonny decided to switch and race with Shannon Hartnett. True to her word, Bonny performed better in the U.S. She took the top spot in the race for the first time. Jean Racine, who raced with brakewoman Shelly Stokes, finished second. Jill Bakken had recovered from her knee injury and took third place with Shauna Rohbock.

The next World Cup event was in Calgary, Alberta, on February 1, 2001. Bonny and I had our best finish ever when we took second place with 1:55.95. During both of our heats, we posted the fastest U.S. team start times—5.90 seconds in both heats. I was growing in strength as a brakewoman and pusher. I still needed to work on my technique, but this greatly increased my confidence. I realized after the first year that I needed to increase my upper body strength. I was used to training my legs. I made plans to spend the next spring and summer in a good strength training program, increasing my upper body strength. Jean Racine and Jen Davidson took first place in that race. Jill Bakken, still not 100 percent after her knee injury, finished fifth with brakewoman Shauna Rohbock.

On February 9, Bonny and I raced in the Women's Bobsleigh World Championships in Calgary, which had competitors from 23 nations. Despite our fast starts of 5:94 and 5:98, we landed in only eighth place. Switzerland's Francoise Burdet won the gold medal, interrupting a season of almost complete domination by Jean Racine and Jen Davidson. Jean and Jen, known to be the top two U.S. women, were having an incredible winning streak against the powerful women from the other nations. They were seen as the Americans to beat.

RETURNING HOME TO RACE

After the world championships in Calgary, Bonny and I returned to our home track in Park City to prepare for the final race of the season. All the teams wanted to do well because this would be the site of the 2002 Winter Olympics. Gaining early confidence on this track could help the drivers mentally and would give the teams an advantage heading into the Olympic year. I was ready to race, but I was more ready to get home to Johnny. Bonny was feeling more comfortable because she had experience on this track. Jean was feeling good about her team's performances. Jill was returning with hopes of making an impact during the last race of the year.

In the first heat of the first World Cup race, Bonny and I broke the start and track records for the Olympic Park and finished in first place by .21 seconds. This is a large margin; it is typical in bobsled to have a slim difference between the various sleds' times. Next, Germany's Sandra Prokoff and her brakewoman, Ulrike Holzner, beat our new start record but not our race time. Jean Racine and Jen Davidson finished in third place, and Jill Bakken and Kristi McGihon finished fifth.

In the second heat, the battle was on for first place and Bonny and I were up for the challenge. Germany's Prokoff and Holzner broke another push record with a 5.33 second start time. They had an excellent drive down the track and finished in 49.05—breaking our previous track record by .02 to take the gold. Bonny and I took second place. Because of our silver medal finish, Bonny improved from sixth to fourth place in the overall driver rankings. Jean and Jen held the third position, and Jill and Kristi finished in fifth place.

In the last World Cup race of the 2000–2001 season, the U.S. women went 1-2-3. It was a great feeling! Jean and Jen finished in first place for the gold medal, Bonny and I took second place for the silver medal, and Jill and Kristi earned the bronze. Jean Racine was the top driver in the United States and the world for the second consecutive year.

FOCUSING ON THE OLYMPICS

After the women's bobsled season ended, each of us in our own way was beginning to focus on the Olympics. We had less than ten months to get ready for the Olympic trials. There were spots for two crews of women bobsledders on the new Olympic team, and the drivers were in keen competition with each other. Jean Racine had had a terrific year, and was relentlessly focused on having the top spot in the U.S. and the world. She seemed unbeatable. But Bonny had a fiercely competitive spirit. She had one goal, Olympic gold, and she was marshaling every resource to reach it—from getting the best equipment to recruiting her own push athlete. Our start times were rivaling those of Jean and Jen. Jill Bakken had always been easygoing, but she had a depth of bobsled experience and a way of showing up again to win. There was no question that the top three sleds would be competing hard for the two places on the Olympic team.

Bonny Warner and I knew we had made great improvements in the past season as a bobsled team—no one could dispute that. But almost anyone around the team could see that some tension was growing between us. My personality and style as an athlete was much more reserved than Bonny's. I was confident in my ability because of my hard work and dedication. Therefore, on race day I was just as relaxed as I had been during training. I've always been laid-back.

On the other hand, Bonny needed to raise her blood pressure, slap herself on the head, and raise her heart rate before each race, and this was fine with me. We had different styles that helped us reach our athletic potential. I was not an athlete who would tell you what I was going to do before I did it. I'm a firm believer that actions speak louder than words. On the other hand, Bonny was much more verbal and constantly talking about her desire to win a gold medal in the Olympic women's bobsled. I accepted her for who she was and hoped that she would learn to accept me for who I was. I was grateful to her for all she did to bring me into bobsled. She loved to show her enthusiasm for the sport and liked to see the same sort of drive and emotion in others. We had very different styles, and this became a problem.

Bonny and I decided to address this by spending more time together. During the summer break, Bonny came to Birmingham and stayed with Johnny and me for a week. We trained and worked out together. I went to California for a week and spent it on weight training and running with Bonny. It gave us a chance to learn more about the other's family and background. We also consciously worked on regular communication and set up times to talk on the phone weekly and sometimes every day. We used e-mail as a means to write to each other about our lives, and to prepare for when we were going to meet with the rest of the women's bobsled team. We were preparing for the Olympic year ahead, and as we improved our personal relationship, my confidence increased. I wanted to do everything I could to make our partnership a success. I wanted to fulfill my lifelong goal of competing in the Olympics, and I used the same skills of steadiness and determination that had served me well in track and field.

COACH LESSONS FOR A LIFETIME

Coach Dewitt Thomas started coaching me when I was nine years old and planted a seed that would grow over the next 19 years. He told me that I would one day be an Olympian, and without reservation I believed him.

Five
COACH LESSONS FOR A LIFETIME

I've been blessed to have coaches who have taught me a lot about how to be a champion in sports as well as how to be a champion in life. In college I became particularly fond of Rod Tiffin as a person and as a coach. He introduced me to the hurdles and the heptathlon and helped me develop into a seven-time All-American. The hurdles were very intimidating at first. I bruised my knees on them at every practice until I learned the proper form and technique. The heptathlon is a two-day series of grueling events; it includes the 110-meter hurdles, 200 meters, javelin, shot put, high jump, 800 meters, and long jump. After competing in the heptathlon I felt like sleeping for two days straight. I wasn't particularly fond of all of the events, but I tried them anyway because Rod thought that this might be another avenue for me to qualify for the Olympic team. I gave it a try because I respected his knowledge, his coaching style, and his ability to help me explore new ideas.

I would have loved for him to coach me throughout my college career, but unfortunately he left UAB and returned to Auburn University, his alma mater, before my senior year. Because of our relationship on and off the track, I thought about transferring in order to pursue my Olympic dreams. Then I thought about my mom and I knew that since I was the only girl in the family, she would be here all by herself. I

thought about Johnny and what it would do to our relationship. I was happily surprised when he told me that he would
transfer if I decided to leave. Fortunately, we both decided to
stay at UAB. We finished our track careers in 1996 and graduated from college shortly after.

Rod and I would meet again a few years later when he
accepted a position at the University of Alabama. He invited
me to be a graduate assistant at UA and said he would also
train me for the 2000 Olympic track-and-field team trials. This
was another tough decision. I wanted to be close to Johnny, but
I knew that since he was a manager at Blue Cross and Blue
Shield of Alabama, there was no way that he could just pack his
things and move to Tuscaloosa. On the other hand, we had
been dating for quite a while and I thought this might be the
motivation he needed to take the next step. Because Tuscaloosa
is only 45 minutes from Birmingham, we could take turns driving back and forth to see each other.

In high school I participated in basketball, volleyball, and
track and field. Out of the three sports I loved basketball the
most. I had never picked up a basketball until my freshman
year at P.D. Jackson Olin High School. My track-and-field
coach, Coach Ford (we called her Mrs. Ford), told me to try out
for the basketball team. All of the students feared Mrs. Ford
because of her work ethic and discipline. Everybody knew that
the 6'1" woman did not play games. When she told us to do
something, we did it. So after a few weeks of practice I began
to learn how to dribble and shoot and eventually made the
team. In the beginning Coach James, the basketball coach, did
not give me many opportunities to play due to my inexperi-
ence. When he finally put me in the game, I caught the ball and
dribbled it a few times before a defender approached me. I
picked the ball up in order to pass it to a teammate, but nobody
was open. I began dribbling again, this time running full-speed

toward the goal. The referee called me for double dribbling and I was immediately put back on the bench. It took a few weeks before Coach James would put me back in the game, but by the end of the season I was in the starting lineup.

If it wasn't for Mrs. Ford, I would have never tried out for the basketball team. And even though she encouraged me to participate in extracurricular activities, she was not too excited when I told her that I had tried out and been chosen to be a cheerleader. Mrs. Ford told me that I did not come to Jackson Olin to be a cheerleader, so the next day I had to quit the squad. She was the toughest track-and-field coach I've ever had. My practices in high school were tougher than they were in college. I didn't understand it at the time, but her discipline helped me to push through any injuries I had. I wanted to be successful for Mrs. Ford because I knew how much she loved us and cared about our athletic futures. Without her pushing me so much, I know I wouldn't have had the work ethic or the belief that I could compete at the college level.

Out of all of my coaches there was only one who made me believe that anything was possible. Coach Dewitt Thomas started coaching me when I was nine years old and planted a seed that would grow over the next 19 years. Coach Thomas told me that I would one day be an Olympian, and without reservation I believed him. He founded the Alabama Striders track club, and I traveled, trained, and roadblocked with them during my early years.

THE ALABAMA STRIDERS

I returned to Birmingham for a few days between my travels for bobsled and was asked by my longtime track coach, Coach Thomas, to speak to his Alabama Striders track team. I thought it was important for me to support a program that had been so instrumental in my life. I looked forward to the opportunity, but I was also a little hesitant to speak to this group. It felt weird thinking back on my days as a Strider, and now I was all grown up and was preparing to return to my old stomping grounds.

One sunny afternoon, I met Coach Thomas and his team at a local track. At the coach's encouragement, the team sat on the bleachers. As the small group of young people listened, I could see the anticipation on their faces. They were looking for some inspiration or something profound from my brief talk.

"I've known Vonetta since she was nine years old," Coach began his introduction. "Throughout her elementary, junior high, and high school years, Vonetta was one of our star athletes on the Alabama Striders (then called the Marvel City Striders). Now she's joined the women's bobsled team and is in training for the 2002 Winter Olympics. I've asked her to come and talk with you for a few minutes this afternoon. So let's give Vonetta Flowers a warm Striders welcome."

I could see their excitement as I stood in front of the group to talk with them. "I don't have a long talk for you or anything complicated," I began. "I've known Coach Thomas and his work with the Striders for many years. We spent long hours together in my training and in my travels to different track events. Coach Thomas built some key strengths in my life, and they have helped me develop into the person I am today. Here's my message to you. Just do what Coach says to do. You may wonder about it, and I'm sure sometimes you will question his preaching to you about this or that." When I mentioned the regular lectures that Coach Thomas gives his athletes, I could see various team members' heads began to nod. They smiled in acknowledgment—they knew exactly what I was talking about. I continued, "But I'm here to tell you this man knows how to help you be the best athlete you can be. Follow his advice and do what he tells you to do."

With that simple word of advice, I was done talking to the Striders. That afternoon as I drove back home, I recalled the first time I saw Coach Thomas and I remembered what he taught me. The lessons from Coach Thomas went well beyond the track and carried into my life.

As a young girl, I always loved to run. The kids where I lived used to race each other up and down the streets to see who was the fastest. This is where I first realized that I had some speed. I didn't know anything about college or what it could do for me, I just enjoyed running. Yet I never ran in a real race until I was in the third grade at Jonesboro Elementary. Our school was typical for an inner-city school—it was somewhat run-down and about 99.9 percent of the students were black.

Coach Thomas had been coaching an inner-city track team since 1983. More than 300 athletes from his team have gone on to college, some to professional sports. With typical modesty, Coach contended that the athletic ability of his youth had something to do with the water in Bessemer, Alabama (Bessemer is a suburb of the city of Birmingham). I believe it is much more than the water. The success of the Striders has more to do with Coach Thomas and his commitment to the youth in Birmingham.

Each fall, Coach Thomas visited the elementary and middle schools throughout the area to test young people in their athletic track abilities. Each kid had a chance to race in the 50-yard dash and test his or her speed against the other students. Because some of the times were so fast, Coach Thomas believed that some of the students had to be at least 12–14 years old. He told us stories about "social promotion" and believed that some of the kids in kindergarten through fourth grade were a lot older than we were and he would have to check their birth certificates in order to place them in the correct age group.

Miss Perry, my physical education teacher, asked us, "Who

wants to race?" Like the other nine-year-olds in my class, I lined up on the mark and listened to the Coach as he yelled, "Ready. Set. Go!" Then everyone raced to the finish line.

Using his stopwatch, the coach recorded my time and name as "V. Jeffery." Because of the number of students, he didn't have time to write down the full name, so he listed the first initial and last name. Jeffery was my maiden name. The Striders practiced at Davis Middle School, and he asked the best athletes to meet him there the next day. The coach assumed one of the older boys in the elementary had captured the fastest time.

That night when he compiled the times, Coach Thomas found that the fastest time at Jonesboro Elementary went to a "V. Jeffery." He assumed the *V* stood for Vincent or Victor or some other boy's name that began with a *V*.

The next day, Coach Thomas met us at the Davis School and asked each of us to sign in. I signed in as "Vonetta Jeffery." When I signed my name, Coach asked me, "Are you V. Jeffery?" At the time, I was very small for my age. He figured that he had made a mistake recording the times. Coach Thomas's Striders already had Tameka Byrd; Coach considered Tameka the best nine-year-old athlete in America.

"Let's check that time again, Vonetta," Coach said. He set up a race between Tameka Byrd and me. Coach Thomas wanted to see how I would stack up against her. In my first competition I lined up against his best athlete and ran until I crossed the finish line. When I looked over, Tameka was crying. Until that point, she had never lost a race in her life. From that point forward, I became the fastest runner in my age group on the Marvel City Striders track team.

OLYMPIC DREAMS

After I joined the track team with Coach Thomas, it quickly became the dominant force in my life. I continued to work hard at my schoolwork, but track was my place to excel. The team expanded my world. The Striders traveled to other states and stayed overnight in hotel rooms. Through track and field, I spent my first night in a hotel bed and learned what it was like to share a room with five other girls. I also took my first long ride on a bus to go to a track meet. I took my first airplane trip with Coach Thomas. I can still recall sitting in the window seat and staring at the small cars and houses and people below the plane. It was an experience that few of my classmates at Jonesboro Elementary had.

In those early days, Coach Thomas recalls my politeness (training from my parents) and my quiet yet obedient nature. I always addressed Coach saying, "Yes, sir" or "No, sir." It was common in the South to address adults in that manner. Even at 10 years old, my parents had taught me respect and had also instilled a strong work ethic in me. Their support helped me to stay focused and it encouraged me to attend practice and to train for the various events, then to compete to the best of my young abilities.

While I was with the Striders, Coach Thomas continually tried me out in new track events. I ran the 100-meter dash, then the 200-meter dash. Coach Thomas introduced me to the 4x400-meter relay and also to the triple jump and the long jump. While some athletes specialized in only one event, Coach Thomas observed that my abilities translated into different sports. I could compete in each of them at the same track meet.

From his experience, Coach knew it was rare to find some-one who could perform well in several different track events. One day he encouraged me and planted the seed of an Olympic dream in my life by saying, "Vonetta, if you keep working at it, maybe one day you could be like Jackie Joyner-Kersee." Olympic great Jackie Joyner-Kersee is often regarded as the best all-around female athlete in the world and the all-time greatest heptathlete. At this young age, I had never heard of Jackie—but I listened to my coach and I latched onto her name. With hard work and training, I believed I had the potential to become an Olympic athlete.

From this early age, I chose to follow a course for my life and athletic career. I didn't realize that I had made a major decision at nine years old. The thought of me going to the Olympics was planted in my mind and I never turned back. My life has involved a series of daily decisions and choices to achieve a level of excellence in my sport. It's hard to explain to other people. You don't simply wake up one morning and become a champion—in anything. Instead, the choices come in small increments.

HOW TO SUCCEED IN ATHLETICS

For me to win in athletics took a combination of factors. First, I had the innate God-given ability of running and jumping. I wasn't a Christian during my growing up years, but the Bible in Romans 12:6 says, "We have different gifts, according to the grace given us." Every single person has been given some ability, and your talent will be distinct from mine. It might be that you have a mathematical mind or you love science or you have an amazing memory or ability to retain information. The key is to be looking for such a gift and recognize it and capitalize on it when you find it. Often other people near you will recognize your gift before you are aware of it. Listen to these people, and if it feels right inside, then follow that dream. When I was only nine years old, Coach Thomas helped me discover my gift in athletics.

Discipline. Discipline was another factor in my athletic achievements. My commitment to discipline began at an early age. Coach Thomas scheduled practices after school. I followed his discipline and came to the practices, ran the laps, and did the exercises. I'll be the first to admit that some days I didn't want to go to practice. I wasn't eager to work up a sweat and do different exercises. Many other things pulled at my attention. Some of my friends wanted to go shopping after school or sit in the mall and watch boys. Or we wanted to watch some television program or simply jump rope and play games with each other. Instead, I chose to follow the discipline of training and practice. Discipline is addressed in the Bible in the Book of Hebrews: "No discipline seems pleasant at the time, but painful. Later on, however, it produces a harvest of righteousness and peace for those who have been trained by it" (Hebrews 12:11). Throughout my childhood and into my adult years, I've felt the pain and unpleasantness of discipline in my training and life, yet I've also experienced the peace that comes from such training.

Diligence. Another virtue that goes hand in hand with discipline is diligence. I consistently followed the instructions of Coach Thomas for my training. Instead of objecting to the number of repetitions or the sprints that we ran in track, I was diligent about showing up, then performing each exercise and each practice. Often people are looking for a quick fix or an easy solution to shoot to the top of their profession. Few people want to stick with something day after day with the necessary diligence. We trained in bad weather and we trained in good weather. If it rained, then we still put on our shoes and workout clothes and practiced. Sometimes we practiced inside, but it was a rare day that we missed a session. Look at these verses from Hebrews and how the writer contrasts diligence as the opposite of laziness: "We want each of you to show this same diligence to the very end, in order to make your hope sure. We do not want you to become lazy, but to imitate those who through faith and patience inherit what has been promised" (Hebrews 6:11–12).

Faithfulness. Another key quality that played into my athletic training was faithfulness. It takes time to develop the necessary skills and muscles to win races. Faithfully I worked out each day and trained for my events. The muscles took time to develop, grow, and become strong. Many young people want to instantly be strong enough to beat others in the race—yet they are unwilling to faithfully move toward a particular goal. Your goal may be outside of athletics, but one of the keys that I've discovered for reaching any goal is faithfully working toward it.

In the New Testament, Jesus told the parable of the talents. A master gave three servants gifts of varying sizes for them to develop; then he left on a journey. Two of the three men doubled their talents while the master was away. To each of these faithful men he said, "Well done, good and faithful servant! You have been faithful with a few things; I will put you in charge of many things. Come and share your master's happiness!" (Matthew 25:23). Notice the emphasis that Jesus makes about being faithful with a few things—as a result your responsibilities will be increased to have responsibility for many things. This type of faithfulness has been true in my life. From an early age, I faithfully worked on my athletics. In a million mini-choices, I could have quit at any moment and not gone to the practices or workouts or the track meets. Instead, I made a different choice and faithfully nurtured my talents and abilities. My lesson about faithfulness has carried into many other areas of my life, but the foundations began in my early track days with Coach Thomas.

Patience. Another quality that I learned early on in my track-and-field career was patience. Today's world almost demands instant success. When we send an e-mail, we expect an instant response, or when we leave someone a message on an answering machine, we expect our message to be instantly returned. We live in an instant-results culture, yet athletics requires patience and consistent practice for the goal ahead. For us to expect instant success is the same as if a farmer planted seeds and expected an instant crop. It's impossible. James encourages patience when he says, "Be patient, then, brothers, until the Lord's coming. See how the farmer waits for the land to yield its valuable crop and how patient he is for the autumn and spring rains. You too, be patient and stand firm, because the Lord's coming is near" (James 5:7–8). From my early days of training, I saw the merit of patient and consistent workouts instead of trying for instant success.

Show up. When Coach Thomas called a practice or needed us somewhere, I showed up. I could have stayed home in front of the television or played with my friends, but instead I made the effort to show up and train with the Striders. These early lessons played into my lifelong track-and-field career and also translated as I changed sports and pursued the bobsled.

Opportunity. It's also critical to recognize an opportunity when you have it and not delay but to seize this opportunity. I love the sound advice the apostle Paul wrote to the Ephesians about this issue saying, "Be very careful, then, how you live— not as unwise but as wise, making the most of every opportunity, because the days are evil" (Ephesians 5:15–16). When Coach Thomas offered me a spot on the Striders, I recognized an unusual opportunity to grow as a person and learn from him and follow his lead. Looking back at those years, Coach Thomas says, "Vonetta had more potential than any other athlete I've ever coached. She was the only athlete that I never found the limits of what she could achieve." It's great to learn from someone like Coach Thomas!

Hard work. I learned a tremendous work ethic from listening to Coach Thomas. I followed each of his instructions without question. As I've heard Coach Thomas tell other people with a hint of exaggeration, "If I asked Vonetta to go through a brick wall, she would ask, 'Which brick wall, Coach?'" At the end of the day, if Coach Thomas asked us to run up a hill 12 times, then I would run up and down the hill 12 times. It was a key part of my work ethic that I followed his instructions and did what the coach requested. It's why when I talk with the Striders today, I always advise them to "Do what Coach Thomas says to do."

Respect. From an early age, my parents taught me to be a respectful person. I never talked back to Coach or questioned his motives. Those early lessons came from my family and I've carried them through with me to this day.

Humility. Occasionally at the beginning of a practice, Coach would gather the entire team for one of his "preaching sessions," as he used to call them. Our team was a talented group of athletes and we would often place as the top team when we went to different competitions. Coach taught us never to brag or boast about our talent but to be humble people. As though he were standing here now, I can hear him saying, "No matter how high you can jump or how fast you can run, at the end of the day, God is going to judge whether you are a nice person or not." Humility counted in the eyes of Coach Thomas. He taught me some lifelong lessons about the value of this virtue. He taught me through what he said and through an event he called "roadblocking."

ROADBLOCKING

After I started working with Coach Thomas and the Striders, the majority of my free time was consumed with track work-outs and competitions. While Coach Thomas did what he could to raise the money for our track uniforms and for travel expenses to the various track events, we knew from our first days with the Striders that track was a costly program.

As Coach Thomas used to tell us, "No finance, no romance." He meant that without the money for our team, we couldn't pay the entry fees for the events or have uniforms or hotel rooms or travel money to get to the events. We competed throughout the country and it was costly to fly or use a bus to get to the events.

Beyond our practice for the team, we participated in something Coach called "roadblocking." The term itself describes the key event—blocking the road. Only a few members of the Striders didn't have to roadblock because their parents paid their expenses on the team. The rest of us wore our red Strider shirts and carried signs that said, "Help Our Track Team." We would surround a particularly busy intersection of the road, and when the light turned red we would walk along the stopped vehicles and hold out our tin cans for a donation. Coach Thomas instructed us, "Give everyone an opportunity to give but don't be a nuisance about it. If the person isn't interested in helping, that's okay. Just thank them for even thinking about it, then walk away."

As we roadblocked, our team learned that some intersections were more productive than others. We had our favorite areas of Birmingham to stand around and look for donations. Not all of the local businesses liked to have a bunch of kids standing at the intersection asking for donations. Sometimes they came out and politely asked us to move to a different part of the city. Other merchants would simply telephone the Birmingham police to register their complaint.

Sometimes, even with our late hours of roadblocking, we didn't manage to get enough funds to stay overnight at a hotel. So we would raise funds up to the last minute in order to rent a bus and buy some food while we were traveling. Other teams were sleeping in their hotel rooms and we were sleeping on the bus. We would play games, sing songs, and laugh until we had tears rolling down our face as the bus driver drove through the night. Then when Coach Thomas had had enough of our playing, he made us go to sleep. It's kind of hard to get a good night's sleep when you're sitting on plastic seats, with little or no air-conditioning, as well as a teammate sitting next to you twisting, turning, and snoring all night. Then there's the smell or smells that suddenly appear. If you've ever been on a long bus ride, it's hard to not smell every different odor that is lingering in the air. Some were the result of people getting too comfortable and deciding to take their shoes off and others were more sporadic. With all of this going on, we had to sleep through the night because Coach Thomas expected us to win the next day. Oddly enough, none of the athletes complained too much because we learned that this was how we had to live in order to survive.

In the morning, we'd stop at a restaurant for breakfast, then drive the final stretch to reach the event. The other competitors would have no idea our team had not spent the night in a local hotel so we could be well rested for the competition. Without saying anything about our travel experiences, we simply warmed up for the event, blocked it out of our minds, and ran hard in every event. The Striders had a very talented team and it was not uncommon for us to sweep an event. After celebrating with supper in a nearby restaurant, our team loaded back on the bus for the return trip.

Roadblocking was not the way most young people would like to spend their time. It was hard work to dodge cars at busy intersections and fund our track trips. Our team didn't have any corporate sponsors or a parents' booster club to raise money. Instead our only means of getting the funds was to roadblock for hours on end. As I look back on those experiences, I appreciate Coach Thomas for teaching us hard work, patience, and sacrifice.

Coach didn't have another job except the Striders. He could have easily worked a regular job and given up on all of us kids. Instead Coach Thomas chose to believe in us and help us reach our goal. He lived to help us reach those goals, and without his support I would not have gone so far in track and field. He believed in my potential when no one else did.

Even today, Coach Thomas recalls those years of working with me and the other kids from the inner city. We worked hard to get to our track meets and understood that this was the only means of getting there. We didn't have the best equipment, shoes, or clothing, but we were a team. And for some of us, this is where we learned how to work together, how to look out for one another, and economics 101. I knew for most of these kids, track and field gave them discipline, it taught them the importance of being on time, and for some it gave us a glimmer of hope.

At that time few of us thought about college because we didn't have those influences in our lives. We simply enjoyed running and having an opportunity to visit other cities. I know for me, track and field became my means to another life beyond what I could experience in my community in Birmingham. Coach Thomas made me believe that even with my humble beginnings I could become an Olympian. I'm not sure how many other kids were training for the Olympics at nine years old or how many were just there to have fun, but at the time I had no reason not to believe that I could one day make him proud of me.

MAYS SISTERS

I spent many days and nights with the Alabama Striders. Over a period of time I created some unique relationships with some of the girls on the team. There were five of us who grew really close to each other and we were basically inseparable. We called ourselves the Mays Sisters. Most people wonder how the name came about, and to be honest I'm not sure who decided to start the group, but after a while all of us had nicknames that ended with May.

Growing up I licked my lips a lot, causing them to become very chapped. For some reason I never carried any ChapStick or Vaseline to relieve the dryness. One particular day, I couldn't find my ChapStick and the girls on the team noticed how ashy (dry) my lips were, and they continued to talk about my lips and how ashy they were all day long. Therefore I became known as *Ashy May*. The other members of the group included:

Felisa Howard (*Falsey May*)—the tip of her front tooth was false.

Erika Gibson (*Moppy May*)—her geri curl was always stringy like a mop instead of curly.

Tameka Byrd (*Muscle May*)—she had bigger muscles than most boys her age.

Katresa Nelson (*Crusty May*)—she received this name for her chocolate-color skin.

Coach Thomas would often refer to the group as the Mays Sisters and knew that when he saw one then the others were close behind. These girls became part of my family and in some ways filled the void of not having a sister. Looking back, it's funny to think of all the good times that we had together and some of the growing pains as well, but I'll never forget what all of these girls meant to me while participating on the Alabama Striders track team. And even now when we see each other, we greet each other in the same manner as we did almost 15 years ago. For a select few, I will always be Ashy May.

I'll be the first to admit my life was not perfect during these growing-up years. I didn't have the best facilities, the proper funding, or the best equipment, but I was involved with a group that helped me believe in myself. I'm fortunate to have been a Strider and to have Coach Thomas as part of my life. As my protector and guide, Coach Thomas helped me and taught me lessons in those early years that I've carried for a lifetime.

FOLLOW THE
OPEN DOOR

I've often heard that the doors of opportunity are always open. Sometimes, it was hard to have faith when a lot of negative things were taking place in my community. But these inspirational words encouraged me and helped me understand that options are readily available for those who seek them.

Six
FOLLOW THE OPEN DOOR

After I failed to make the U.S. Olympic track-and-field team at the 2000 trials, I had time to reflect on my life and what I thought was important. It appeared that my athletic career was over and I had failed to live out my childhood dream. I didn't know how I was going to respond, given the fact that I had chased this goal basically all of my life. I had reached a point in my career when I had to decide if I wanted to put my family on hold for another four years or finally step into a new world by becoming a mother. Even though Johnny and I had already talked about starting a family if I didn't make the team, it was hard to think that all of the hard work, the dreaming, the anticipation was over.

I believe that most athletes who pursue an Olympic dream are doing so because they feel they have an extraordinary gift to compete at the highest level. For most, the opportunity to represent their country comes around only once or twice. Only a select few have the chance to sustain their top physical performance for more than 10 years. With this being the case, I felt that my time was done, having failed to qualify in 1996 in Atlanta, Georgia, and in 2000 at the Olympic trials in Sacramento, California.

At about the time I was getting ready to feel sorry for myself, it seemed that a golden opportunity presented itself. Hundreds of athletes passed by the poster that Bonny had put on the bulletin board encouraging track-and-field athletes to continue their dream of competing in the Olympics. Fewer than ten people actually showed up for the bobsled tryout on the day that Johnny and I answered the "help wanted" ad. The number of athletes who came out did not surprise me, but now that I look back on it I realize that if I had not been open to new ideas and willing to take a risk, then I wouldn't have realized my dream.

I've often heard that the doors of opportunity are always open. Sometimes, growing up in Birmingham, it was hard to have faith in those words when a lot of negative things were taking place in my community. But these inspirational words encouraged me and helped me understand that options are readily available for those who seek them. It didn't mean that there's equal opportunity for everyone, but that there's always an alternate choice. For me, making the right choices started early in life.

EARLY DECISIONS

I attended A.G. Gaston Middle School in Birmingham from the fifth to eighth grade. There I sang in the choir, I was on the volleyball team, and I also participated in track and field. Mrs. Dillworth, the choir instructor, taught us a wide range of songs and we traveled within the city competing at local competitions. The first year I was grouped with the sopranos and the second year I sang with the altos. I enjoyed spending time with my friends and pretending that I had a great voice. Mrs. Dillworth knew the truth. She always stuck me in the middle of the group in order to drown my voice. I guess that explains why she never asked me to sing a solo.

During these years I began to see a lot of physical changes in myself, as well as in most of my friends. These were awkward times, and for some of us it was difficult to talk to our parents about what we were feeling, so we dealt with a lot of emotions internally. I remember boys trying to talk to me and often they would pass notes during class asking if I wanted to be their girlfriend. Sometimes I would show the notes to my friends, but most of the time I would just throw them in the trash. I didn't want to have a bad reputation, nor did I want to disappoint my mom or Mrs. Ford (the strong-willed coach I told you about in chapter 5) by becoming a teenaged mother. So I decided that I didn't need a boyfriend until later in life.

Mrs. Ford made it clear that we would have plenty of time for boys once we got older. Therefore, on our track trips she would make sure that the girls sat in the front of the bus and the boys sat in the rear. She helped us focus on what was important and helped us to see the big picture. While most of the girls listened to and respected Mrs. Ford, there were always a few who had to learn the hard way. I knew that I wasn't going to be one of those girls who made a mistake and lived to regret it the rest of her life. Unfortunately, I did have a friend (who was not on the track team) who became pregnant in the seventh grade. She had to miss one year of school and returned the next year, but this time she had greater responsibilities besides trying to pick out which outfit she was going to wear. I wish that Kim had had someone like Mrs. Ford in her life.

I've always been a person who cared about other people's feelings and how they felt about me. I didn't want to let those close to me down by doing something that would embarrass me or my family. And I wanted my three brothers to act the same way. Unfortunately, my brother, Jimmie Jr., was not as excited about the idea. He was four years older than I was and was in high school when he decided to start smoking. I would catch him smoking in the alley between the house and the corner store. Every time he saw me coming he knew that he was going to be in trouble when he got home because there was no amount of begging and pleading that would stop me from telling on him. I didn't know the effects of smoking and what it was doing to his body. I just hated watching him hurt himself by trying to be cool. I also knew that it could lead to something more serious.

The Decision to Continue

By my junior year in high school I had already received two MVP awards at the state track meet held in Selma, Alabama. I was looking forward to my junior year with hopes of returning a team title to Birmingham. I continued to play basketball in the off-season and I was falling more and more in love with the game. I learned how to dribble and run at the same time and had developed better accuracy shooting the ball. My confidence grew as I went from warming the bench to being a key player on the team. All was going well until a routine layup turned into a night in the emergency room.

I saw an opportunity to steal the ball from my opponent, and in less than a second she watched the ball leave her hand as I sprinted toward our goal with it. I jumped off my left leg, I had the ball in my right hand, and I performed one of the basic shots that I had done hundreds of times. As the ball passed through the net I landed on my right leg and immediately felt a pop behind my knee. I fell to the floor and began crying. The coaches ran over and helped me off the court. We didn't have an athletic trainer due to limited funds, so the coaches looked at it and decided to do what most coaches recommended for strains and bruises: they put some ice on it and had me elevate my leg. Luckily, it was close to halftime and I wouldn't miss much of the game as long as the injury was not too serious. After 15 minutes of icing the area had become completely numb and I either blocked out the pain or the ice prevented me from noticing it.

When the second half started I was in the starting lineup, still in pain and determined to help my team win the game. The ball was tipped and I began running down the court and it happened again. At that point I realized that I had severely damaged my leg. After the game the coach rushed me to the emergency room, and that's when we discovered that I had torn my ACL (anterior cruciate ligament).

The next day I visited Children's Hospital to meet with Dr. Garth. He informed me that it would take six months to recover from this type of surgery. He explained that it was not mandatory to have the surgery immediately, but it would be necessary if I wanted to continue competing. He told me that I could use a knee brace in order to stabilize it until I made up my mind. There was no question whether or not to have the surgery; the problem was that it happened at a bad time. The outdoor track-and-field season was only a few months away. I decided to try and run with my knee brace and postpone the surgery until the season was over.

My junior year in high school was the most challenging year I faced. I was the defending champion in the long jump, the triple jump, the 200 meters, and the 400 meters. When I arrived at the state track meet, most of the athletes had already heard of my injury and were ready to take their position on top of the podium. I had not qualified in the long jump or triple jump due to the fact that I could not place any pressure on my leg. Therefore, the only events that I participated in were the 200 and 400. Even with the pain, the knee brace, and the torn ACL, I was still able to win the 200 and place third in the 400 meters. I was glad that I chose to continue competing even though I had an injury. Mrs. Ford's teachings had played a role in my decision and I believed that I would make a full recovery after the surgery and months of rehab.

In 1992 I had a lot to prove to myself, my high school

coaches, and the college coaches who were recruiting me. I knew that some people had become a little skeptical about my abilities due to my injury. That's why I worked extra hard to make sure that I was ready to compete in the 6A state track-and-field championships. It was sort of a bittersweet ending to my high school career. I wanted so much to attend my high school prom and experience the whole process of buying a dress, taking pictures, going out to an expensive restaurant, and hanging out with my friends. Instead I found myself running laps at the track preparing for my final state championships.

I was very pleased with my final performance at the Alabama state track-and-field championships. Over the summer I trained very hard to become stronger than I was before. Once again I was able to win the 200, the 400, the long jump, and the triple jump. I was named state MVP for the third time and was ready to start seriously considering where I would attend college. I would later learn that Johnny also attended the state meet, as he qualified in several events while attending Berry High School, which was only 20 minutes from P.D. Jackson Olin. Based on pictures and home video, we found later that we had attended several meets together, but we wouldn't meet until our freshman year at UAB.

THE RIGHT CHOICE

During my senior year of high school, I knew I was bound for college. Because of my track-and-field accomplishments, a number of track coaches in the Southeastern Conference tried to recruit me to their programs. I visited several different programs. Each one offered a full athletic scholarship to the college. I heard from the University of Alabama, the University of Georgia, Mississippi State, and Ole Miss (the University of Mississippi). As a young person, it was a difficult choice for me.

I could have gone to any of these fine institutions, and many of these coaches were shocked with my selection of the University of Alabama at Birmingham (UAB). UAB had no depth in their women's track and field, and they had no outstanding facilities and no nationally recognized relay team.

When it comes down to it, I'm from Birmingham and I wanted to go to college where I could stay close to my mom. UAB gave me the opportunity to receive a college education and to participate in track and field. As a young person, I simply followed this open door and followed my heart. Many changes in my life occurred in my time at UAB—including meeting the loves of my life, Johnny Flowers and Jesus Christ. It might not have happened at another university.

Some people may wonder at my choice of a college, but I felt grateful to have the opportunity to go to college. My mother graduated from high school, but my father never did. My father had to quit school in order to help support the family. I'm sure he would have preferred finishing school versus working all day. Many young people take their high school graduation for granted. Because I had a parent who didn't graduate, I knew firsthand the special nature of my graduation. And after my high school graduation, I became the first member of my immediate family to attend college and work for a college degree.

My life journey continued as a series of choices. My college years at UAB would hold more for me than I could imagine.

Above: Vonetta, age 10, slows down long enough to take a Fourth of July picture with her cousin Ann.

Right: Vonetta and her mom enjoy an afternoon cooking in the kitchen.

Above: Vonetta poses with her brother Eric.

Above, right: Vonetta at age nine, when Coach Dewitt Thomas discovered her running ability.

Above: Vonetta smiles at a track meet in Indiana, just weeks before the Olympic track-and-field trials in 2000. She had just recovered from ankle surgery.

Left: Running and jumping are fine; it's the thought of landing that makes Vonetta frown. As a track athlete, Vonetta competed in the 100-meter dash, 200-meter dash, triple jump, long jump, hurdles, and the relays.

Vonetta married her college sweetheart, Johnny Flowers, on
September 25, 1999.

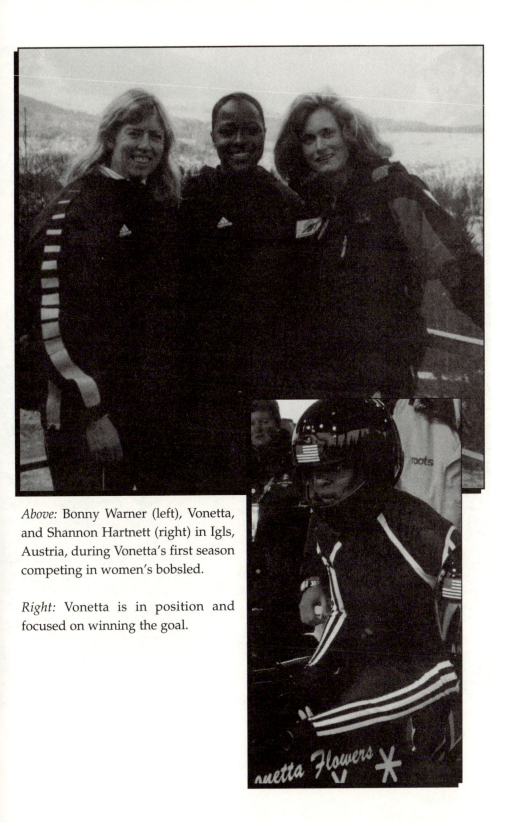

Above: Bonny Warner (left), Vonetta, and Shannon Hartnett (right) in Igls, Austria, during Vonetta's first season competing in women's bobsled.

Right: Vonetta is in position and focused on winning the goal.

Above: Bonny Warner (front) and Vonetta give a powerful push to their Bo-Dyn sled during a World Cup competition.

Right: After their gold medal victory, Jill Bakken and Vonetta Flowers made lots of public appearances and met many famous people, among them Al Roker of the *Today* show.

Golden girl Vonetta Flowers is presented with a torch from Coca-Cola during her welcome home celebration at the University of Alabama at Birmingham.

THE TWO LOVES
OF MY LIFE

*One of the main benefits of being a Christian is to know
God is on my side. He has a master plan for my life and
as long as I trust and depend on Him, He'll help me make
wise decisions. The battle is already won.*

Seven
THE TWO LOVES OF MY LIFE

New Year's Day 2001 was a joyous time in my life. Johnny and I had celebrated Christmas and welcomed in another year. The New Year always reminds me of the opportunity to begin fresh with a renewed energy and new opportunities.

Only a few weeks earlier in December, Bonny Warner and I had completed the first half of the season with a bronze medal at the track in Igls, Austria. Even though the season started kind of rocky, it felt good to medal in the fourth World Cup event of the season. Now for the Christmas/New Year's holidays, I was back in Birmingham training for the second half of the women's bobsled season, which was scheduled to continue in Calgary, Alberta, in early January.

Besides my work with the women's bobsled team, I continued as assistant track coach at the University of Alabama at Birmingham. While I was home, I wanted to make sure I checked on my "girls." I missed seeing them every day, watching them grow, and just being a part of their daily lives. One afternoon, I drove over to the campus.

As I arrived, in my mind I returned to those first days on the campus. While I had spent all my life in Birmingham, I had never lived away from home. In the fall of 1992, I moved into Camp Hall, which was a coed dorm on the 16,000-student campus.

College brought me a new sense of freedom and adventure.

125

I enjoyed the challenge of my new classes combined with my regular workouts with the track team. The team was relatively small, with only about three or four women on the team. As we worked out, I got to know a cute guy who was also a freshman on the team, Johnny Flowers. Besides his good looks, Johnny had a unique sense of humor. Almost instantly I loved his jokes and knew that he was one of the few people who had ever come into my life who could make me laugh. It was infectious. Every Wednesday night, Johnny and I had a chance to get better acquainted because the track team ate dinner together and the group setting provided an easygoing environment.

I didn't see Johnny in my life in a romantic way—at least at first. He was involved in a different relationship and I was also going out with someone. Still, it was obvious that Johnny liked being with me from the way he acted and a few of the things he said.

During this period, I was working as a hostess at a local restaurant in Birmingham called Wings. I was driving an old Toyota Corolla that I called my "Jag," because this was my dream car. Well, one night the Jag wouldn't start. It typically took about 5–10 minutes to get it started, but this night I had stomped on the clutch and pressed the gas for almost 20 minutes before I decided to call for help. I was stuck and unsure who to call for help at 11:30 P.M. I knew my mom would come and get me, but at that time of night she was sound asleep and I didn't really want to wake her. Then I thought of Johnny, and he gladly came and rescued me from this situation.

Later, Johnny told me about what was going on in his head and heart during this time. He was attracted to me physically and had thought about asking me out, but he didn't want to ask until he was sure I would say yes. He confessed that he had been sending signals, but I either refused to respond or was working on his patience. The fact that I didn't let him know that I liked him made him more determined to talk to me. We worked out together at the track and Johnny was impressed that regardless of the difficulty of the workout, I was always able to maintain my coolness and I never complained. As Johnny tells it, "Anyone who could endure our workouts in the 110-degree weather and not complain, I knew she had to be either an exceptional athlete or just extremely cool. In either case, I wanted to get to know Vonetta and didn't stop chasing her until she agreed."

Over the next few months, I discovered that Johnny was a gentleman, and he continued to make me laugh. We both lived in the Camp Hall dormitory, but on different floors. One night a Michael Jackson special was going to be on HBO, and I knew Johnny had HBO while I did not have it in my room. I asked if I could come down and watch the special with him, not knowing that he was reading more into it. When I arrived the smell of homemade lasagna was seeping out of his room. I wasn't quite sure if he made it or had his mom bring it over. In either case, I was impressed that he went to the trouble of preparing a meal. I was expecting to pop a frozen pizza in the oven.

I was amazed to find a guy who could cook—even if it was just one dish—and was surprised that he actually used seasoning salt to give it a nice flavor. Dinner was great, and we enjoyed the show together. As we sat in his room, Johnny turned to me and asked me officially to be his girlfriend. In response, I gave him a kiss—and that's how our relationship started. Johnny has a slightly different version.

The relationship began to blossom. We would jog to practice together, we sat by each other at the study hall sessions, and shared many meals over the next few years. The team traveled to different competitions and often we had to stay overnight in a hotel. I remember our first trip with the team and the night that Phil gave Johnny the man-to-man talk.

One night Johnny, our friends Tammy and Chip, and I were sitting around talking before it was time to go to bed. As Johnny left the room, the head UAB track coach, Phil Schoensee, yelled across the breezeway to get Johnny's attention. Apparently Phil had been watching the door to make sure that the boys slept in their room and that the girls slept in our room. Phil was a very easygoing coach, and I don't remember him ever raising his voice except to cheer us on. He was sitting near the window playing his guitar when Johnny walked in. At the time, I couldn't hear the conversation because Phil played the guitar while he talked, but Johnny later told me about it.

He started in very general terms by talking about why he recruited Johnny to run track and what he expected from him at his first collegiate indoor track-and-field meet. Then the conversation got a little weird because Phil started talking to Johnny about relationships. Coach wasn't smiling but was completely serious when he said, "I brought Vonetta on this team and worked hard to get her. I expect great things from her competition here at UAB." Phil basically told him that he had high hopes for my career and he didn't want to see good talent wasted due to raging hormones. This was Coach Phil's way of telling Johnny that he would be watching him. The conversation ended with Johnny promising not to do anything that would hurt the team's chances of winning a conference championship, and with those words Phil continued to sing and play his guitar as he sat in the window, making sure Johnny kept his word and went back to his own room.

Throughout my college years and beyond, Johnny has always been there for me. We've trained together and competed together and were with each other all the time. We were best friends. I'll admit that it was part of a test that I put him through in the beginning, but I had to take my time and find out if he was serious about me or was just looking for someone to hang out with. Once I learned his intentions, I began to fall in love with him and felt that I should introduce him to my family.

One night my mom Barbara Jeffery, my brother Jimmie Jeffery Jr., his wife Sonya, my youngest brother Eric, and my nephew Tez all came to visit me at the dorm. I knew that my brothers would check him out at first and not really say too much. But I wanted my mom to finally meet the guy I had been dating for months. Hopefully she would like him, because I felt he would one day be her future son-in-law. When Johnny stopped by, I introduced him to the family and shortly after we were all laughing and having a good time. By the end of the night he had been formally introduced to my family and I knew that he would fit in just fine.

On weekends, Johnny came home with me and ate with my family. Other weekends, I would go home with Johnny and eat with his family. Every day we continued to grow in our relationship as a couple. Johnny is the love of my life and a constant in the middle of many changes of my life.

MY OTHER GREAT LOVE

While college, my track career, and my love life were good, I felt something was missing in my life. I had no spiritual connection, and faith in God wasn't part of my life. Our family rarely went to church except for Christmas and Easter. Sunday in our family was another day to rest, relax, and get ready for the upcoming week. It wasn't part of my routine to attend church.

Johnny was the son of a preacher. He had talked about church so much that it made me tired of hearing his stories. He claims that they went to church seven days a week when he was growing up. I'm not sure if it was that much, but by the time he entered college, he decided that it was time to take a break. It wasn't until his junior year that he started attending church again on a regular basis.

When we weren't traveling with the team, Johnny and I would visit different churches in Birmingham. After several weeks of church hunting, Johnny decided that he wanted to go to a particular church because he liked the teaching. He joined the church and went through the new members' class, which took him a long time to complete due to our travel schedule. But he finally completed the classes and was happy that he had joined the church. I was a little hesitant about joining a church; I felt better after going to church, singing songs, and praying to God, but I wasn't ready to make a commitment. Johnny didn't put any pressure on me, so I decided to wait until it felt right for me.

While in college, one of my high school friends, Sylterica Pams, invited me to attend her church, Faith Chapel Christian Center, a nondenominational church in Birmingham. I went to one of the Sunday services and immediately knew it was different from any church I'd ever attended.

The difference was evident from the minute we drove into the parking lot. Almost like at a professional sporting event, parking attendants guided our car to the next available spot and we parked in an orderly manner, and it felt good to see smiling faces giving us what felt like personal attention even before we entered the church.

Then when we walked into the church, people were friendly and an usher guided us into a specific seat. They didn't allow us to sit in the back or off to the side; we were guided to a specific seat and they filled in the entire church from the front row. The back rows of the church and other special sections were reserved for latecomers.

As I walked into the church, the choir singing in the front caught my attention. The service had already started and the combination of an organ with guitar and drums made the service very upbeat. There was something exciting about this church. The choir seemed happy as they wore their festive-colored shirts and blouses as they rocked from side to side with the music. I easily learned some of the songs like:

> *Bread of Life sent down from Glory,*
> *Many things You were on earth,*
> *A holy king a carpenter,*
> *You are the living Word.*

The clear and Scripture-based songs were moving and heartfelt. After the service ended, I caught myself humming these tunes that I had heard on the radio plenty of times.

As I looked around, everyone was carrying a Bible. Pastor Michael D. Moore led the service. I loved how Pastor Mike used real-life stories and simply talked to me. Throughout his teaching, I could see people taking notes and writing down the points and the Scripture references. Turning pages was the sound that echoed around the church when Pastor Mike talked about a particular verse from the Bible. The people in the audience were paying close attention to each point.

I've been to some churches where you can barely understand the pastor because of the screaming and yelling. Everything about Faith Chapel was done in order. The overall purpose of this church is captured in their mission statement: "Faith Chapel Christian Center is a ministry of excellence, impacting nations with a practical message of faith, empowering Word-hungry people to experience and exemplify the God-quality of life." A large sign on the back of the sanctuary told me immediately who the people wanted to be: "Faith Chapel Christian Center, the most loving church in all the world." I could feel the love from the people around me.

At the end of each service, Pastor Mike gives an altar call with four possible responses: (1) to accept Christ in your life, (2) to rededicate your life to Jesus Christ, (3) to be filled with the Holy Spirit, or (4) to explore church membership. I felt a tugging at my heart to go to the front, but at that particular service I didn't go to the front.

I knew I had found a spiritual home for my life and came back the next Sunday. After several weeks, I brought Johnny. As the son of a preacher, Johnny knew a great deal more than I knew about church. He was also impressed with the orderly yet biblical approach from Pastor Mike. Soon, Johnny and I were both going to Faith Chapel on a regular basis. But Johnny was not excited about going through a new members' class again.

The church had a series of core values, and Pastor Mike's teaching regularly built these values into my life. For example, the church values teaching and the practicality of God's Word. They value excellence and hold to the belief that God deserves our best (Daniel 6:1–3). Another core value for Faith Chapel that resonated with my life was the value placed on integrity of heart. They hold to the belief that the Word of God will not produce a dishonest heart. Integrity and honesty had always been a key part of my career in track and field. I was encouraged to know I could turn to the Scriptures for a Bible-based reason for my actions.

Also, I desired not just to come to a church service but also to grow in my faith. Another emphasis of Faith Chapel is the importance of small groups. In their teaching, they said, "We value small group ministry as one of the most effective means of building relationships, stimulating spiritual growth, reaching the lost and unchurched, and developing leaders" (Mark 6:39–44).

Because I love to laugh, it was fascinating to me that Pastor Mike also emphasized the value of humor. Proverbs 15:13 says,

"A happy heart makes the face cheerful, but heartache crushes the spirit," and Proverbs 17:22 says, "A cheerful heart is good medicine, but a crushed spirit dries up the bones." Pastor Mike taught that being cheerful keeps us healthy, and serving God can be fun.

Also I learned about the importance of prayer from Pastor Mike. He taught that prayer is the foundation of every successful endeavor in the kingdom of God. There are many relevant Bible verses to illustrate such an emphasis, but I like the encouragement from the apostle Paul in Philippians 4:6–7: "Do not be anxious about anything, but in everything, by prayer and petition, with thanksgiving, present your requests to God. And the peace of God, which transcends all understanding, will guard your hearts and your minds in Christ Jesus." Prayer was going to be an important key in the development of my spiritual relationship.

At church I also learned the spiritual value of successful living in every area of my life—whether in athletics or at a job or in my home. Pastor Mike teaches us that a platform of success is the best platform from which a person can witness for Jesus Christ. When God spoke to Joshua as the new leader of the children of Israel, He told him, "Do not let this Book of the Law depart from your mouth; meditate on it day and night, so that you may be careful to do everything written in it. Then you will be prosperous and successful. Have I not commanded you? Be strong and courageous. Do not be terrified; do not be discouraged, for the LORD your God will be with you wherever you go" (Joshua 1:8–9). As we keep our mind and heart in the Word of God, the Bible, then we will follow God's truth instead of the world's way.

Also from attending Faith Chapel, I learned the value of order in the church. They even made order a key value, saying, "We value order and hold to the belief that organization does not hinder the free working of the Holy Spirit but rather releases Him to help and operate in our midst in a greater measure."

Finally, another key value I learned was the importance of being on time and prompt to the services and meetings. As Pastor Mike said, "We believe that being late is a sign of disrespect for the person or persons with whom you are meeting." Romans 12:11 says that we should not lag in diligence. I knew it was basic common sense, but so often many people straggled late into church services without an emphasis on this value.

After several weeks of attending the church, when Pastor Mike gave the altar call, I walked forward for church membership. When I came forward, a man and a woman met with me and prayed with me. Then I was enrolled in the church membership class. It wasn't a onetime event but a series of 15 classes. The same class was held a couple of different times during the week. Because of the flexibility, it was relatively easy to get to the class each week.

These classes were each on a major area of the Christian life so that the members of the church understand some of the key areas of the local church. Each week covered a different topic, such as the purpose of the local church, and another week we examined the distinction between God's view and Satan's view of the local church. Another class was on why a Christian should join a Bible-teaching church, and another class taught us how to select a good church. In each class, the Bible was our textbook and I learned a great deal about how to live as a Christian. It's not just a set of rules and dos and don'ts, but the Christian life is based on my personal relationship with Jesus.

A LIFE-CHANGING DECISION

During one of the early classes, I was asked if I had a personal relationship with Jesus, and because I didn't have one, I responded, "No." They asked if I would like to know Jesus personally and I said, "Yes." A couple of people prayed with me and I accepted Jesus Christ as my Savior.

Before I became a Christian, I didn't feel like a bad person, but I was lost without Christ because I had never accepted Him into my life. That day at the membership class, I made a life-changing decision.

The decision meant more than going to church or studying the Bible on a regular basis. It meant that day in and day out, I was going to follow the heart of God and the footsteps of Jesus. My Bible became more than a book that I carried to church on Sundays. The Bible came to life and held spiritual nourishment and I turned to it often for strength.

I had people around me who would drink and smoke, and after I became a Christian, a believer in Jesus, I became more verbal than I ever was in the past. I would speak up and tell people that it wasn't right—not in a judgmental way, but in a simple way of telling the truth in love. I was much more aware of my conscience, and I felt guilty if I did nothing or said nothing. God and the Holy Spirit were working in my life and heart—as they continue to do every day.

After the membership classes, I began to go to a small-group Bible study once a week in addition to church on Sunday. The Bible became a part of my daily life, and reading it each day for inspiration and encouragement has been a part of my routine and life.

Besides daily prayer and Bible study, Pastor Mike has also taught me about the need to give back to others. One of the ways I can grow in my spiritual life is through my involvement in one of the many ministries of the local church. I took an active role in the activities ministry. We planned the major activities for the church and I was also involved in a play that we performed for the kids in the children's ministry. Being involved has given me another opportunity to give back to others and also to grow in how I verbalize my faith and spiritual life.

TRUSTING GOD IN EVERYDAY LIFE

When it comes to my everyday life and my career in athletics, one of the main benefits of being a Christian is to know God is on my side. He has a master plan for my life and as long as I trust and depend on Him, He'll help me make wise decisions. The battle is already won. In my younger days, I never prayed on a regular basis or asked Him for direction. The only time I would ever pray was out of a need or because I was in trouble and needed help as soon as possible. In that troublesome situation, I made promises to God that I knew I wouldn't keep as long as He got me out of my mess. I used prayer for selfish needs.

Now I realize that God is there for me all the time. I've learned how to communicate with Him and listen when He speaks. Also, I have discovered that I am under less stress because I realize that He can help me handle any of my problems. My confidence and strength and courage have increased because I can read the Bible and draw on the strength of others and feel encouraged because of other miracles that He's performed in the lives of the people in the Bible.

College brought two loves into my life that became the true loves of my life. One of them is my husband, Johnny Flowers. He is my constant guide and protector and friend. During my college days, our friendship grew into something that remains special and unique. The other love of my life is Jesus Christ. Through my personal relationship with Jesus, this love affects my life and how I handle my athletics. Instead of leaning on just my own power or strength, I'm able to turn to God for my spiritual and physical strength. Both of these loves are critical to my everyday life.

My college years were special to me and an important part of my life. Throughout college, I competed in track and field predominantly in the 100 meters, 200 meters, long jump, and the triple jump, plus the relay races. A majority of the team only competed in one or maybe two events. As with the Alabama Striders, I competed in a number of different events at the same time.

My track career continued to find success. Because I was blessed with the opportunity to win my different events, I became a vital part of the team's success. Even when I was sick I still wanted to compete. In one event in particular, I was ill with the flu but insisted on competing. I was scheduled to compete in the 60 meters, the 60-meter hurdles, the 200 meters, the long jump, the triple jump, and the 4x4 relay.

While I didn't feel good, I still managed to compete in some of the events—and I even won the long jump. After the long jump, I faced pure exhaustion and had to be carried off the field. So much for that particular competition, because I was finished until I recovered from the flu.

By the time I graduated from UAB, I was one of the university's most decorated athletes, with 35 conference titles, with victories in the Penn Relays and the Olympic Festival, and as UAB's first seven-time All-American.

It was a proud day for me and my family and friends like Coach Thomas when I crossed the stage at the University of Alabama at Birmingham and received my diploma. In terms of my personal achievement, it was another milestone. Few members of my immediate family had graduated from high school, but I was the first to graduate from an institution of higher learning—college.

As I wore my cap and gown and graduated, I was aware that throughout my elementary school years, high school days, and then college, I made a million individual, small choices. At any point I could have given up and quit. I could have stopped my track-and-field career. I could have stopped training. I could have stopped going to my classes and studying and taking tests. At each juncture, in faith, I continued ahead.

I've learned that the way of faith often involves the narrow and difficult choices of life. When Jesus was on earth, He talked with His disciples about the kingdom of God and how to enter it.

> "He said to them, 'Make every effort to enter through the narrow door, because many, I tell you, will try to enter and will not be able to. Once the owner of the house gets up and closes the door, you will stand outside knocking and pleading, "Sir, open the door for us." But he will answer, "I don't know you or where you come from." Then you will say, "We ate and drank with you, and you taught in our streets." But he will reply, "I don't know you or where you come from. Away from me, all you evildoers!" There will be weeping there, and gnashing of teeth, when you see Abraham, Isaac and Jacob and all the prophets in the kingdom of God, but you yourselves thrown out. People will come from east and west and north and south, and will take their places at the feast in the kingdom of God. Indeed there are those who are last who will be first, and first who will be last.'"
> —Luke 13:24–30

From following Jesus Christ, I've learned (and I'm learning) the importance of this relationship and how it helps me make the right choices and have the faith and courage for everyday living. I had no idea how important the spiritual part of my life would become with the difficulties and obstacles in the days ahead as I faced the Olympics and the women's bobsled team.

A Season of Hope

There was no question about my desire to go to the Olympics, but I had doubts about our security. I could hear Pastor Mike's voice in my mind, saying, "Fear or faith." And with those words I gained the confidence I needed. I refused to stay at home and allow the terrorists to kill my dream.

Eight
A SEASON OF HOPE

A new season for an athlete is always full of great optimism and anticipation. For me, the 2001–2002 bobsled season fit both of these feelings. I trained all summer without suffering any injuries. It had been a long time since I was able to compete without being hampered by some type of nagging injury. I had been in contact with Bonny and I knew she was happy with her training. We were both excited to be returning to the ice with hopes of making history by being part of the inaugural year of Olympic women's bobsled. Just being on the team meant that our sport had come full circle. I remember reading about the days when women were not even allowed to participate because the men thought it was too dangerous. Even though it had taken a long time, women bobsledders were finally accepted into the bobsledding community. It was our time to show the doubters what women could do and there was no bigger stage or better place to introduce women's bobsled than at the 2002 Olympics in Salt Lake City, Utah.

While Johnny and I were in Birmingham, we tried to get some local support for my competition. Considering that many people in and around Alabama had never even heard of bobsled, it is nothing short of amazing that we found any support at all. Ty Williams, a former Blue Cross and Blue Shield manager who worked with Johnny, thought it would be a good idea for us to speak to the Shades Valley Rotary Club. It turned out to be a great opportunity for me to talk to a group of men and women who could help support our cause. Ross O'Brien owned a Web site company and agreed to donate his talent to develop a Web site—www.vonettaflowers.com. Sperry Snow, co-owner of Barton-Clay Fine Jewelry, and several other members made personal contributions. Ethan White with Eskridge, White, and Associates helped me by providing the physical therapy I needed to be in prime competitive shape. Also, AIT Worldwide Logistics provided sponsorship through the "Adopt-An-Athlete" program.

The most sizeable contribution would come to me through General Motors' "Team Behind the Team" program, which supported Olympic hopefuls by giving them new automobiles to relieve some of the financial burden of preparing for competition. Their donation of a black 2002 Chevy Malibu to me gave Johnny's overused Honda a much-deserved rest. The best part about getting the car was that it was equipped with air-conditioning, since our old Honda's AC had given out many months earlier.

Beginning my second full season in bobsled, I started to understand and be involved with some of the politics and relationships that shaped the sport. The United States Bobsled and Skeleton Federation (USBSF) is the national governing body for the United States in the international amateur sports of bobsledding and skeleton. There are approximately 500 members of this group, which includes athletes of all ages, coaches, officials, parents, and even fans who are working to strengthen the sport.

One of the complications of the sport is that the athletes and coaches set the specific rules for the bobsled. One of these rules allows the driver of each crew to choose their own brakeperson. The men have used this process for years with some success. Coaches can give input, but they don't make the actual decision about who a driver will slide with. Drivers like this rule because it means they can't be stuck with a coach's bad decision—the driver is free to go out and get the person they feel is best for the job. But it creates some other dynamics. The longer a driver and brakewoman slide together, and the more they become known by the media, the more shocking it becomes if a driver chooses another brakewoman. The drivers often have to choose between their current good relationship with a brakewoman and the possibility of going faster with another person pushing. Bobsledders are just like other athletes—we want to win races and we want to have great relationships. It can be hard if we feel we have to choose between the two.

All of us on the team knew that Bonny felt like the Lone Ranger when it came to the team. If she didn't get what she needed from the coaches or the system, she'd go out and get it herself. When she was stuck with a lousy sled, she got the Eagle's Club to finance a new Bo-Dyn for the team. When she needed better equipment, she invested in personal runners. When the USBSF provided only minimal funding, she developed a support system from friends and coworkers. She didn't want to question whether she was getting the proper coaching, so she hired her own coach. Bonny promised to leave no stone unturned in making sure her team was fully prepared. Nor did she want to wonder if she had the best brakewoman, so she recruited me and Shannon Hartnett and brought us into the sport at her own expense. But there are many complexities in the sport, and a variety of factors that are beyond our control. The playing field is rarely level. The reality is that sometimes a person can have all of the right equipment and still lose.

For the new season, Jill Bakken was paired with Shauna Rohbock, Jean Racine was teamed up with Jen Davidson, and Bonny and I made up the final team in contention. There were a few other drivers, but barring a disaster, everyone close to bobsled knew that two out of these three sleds would represent the U.S. at the Olympics. The possibility of making the Olympic team was a reality. Bonny and I needed to beat one of the other two teams in order to have a chance to represent our country. These odds were better than any of the other odds I had faced in 1996 and in 2000. With the season just a few months away, the U.S. bobsled team headed north in August 2001 to train at Canada Olympic Park (COP).

When I ran the 100 meters in track, I had to focus on my start, accelerate during my drive phase, then use every ounce of energy to run as fast as I could. Bobsled is a little more complicated. In bobsled, my teammate and I have to time our initial hit. I have to push, run on my toes, and make sure my body is pushing the sled forward instead of applying down force on the sled. Then at just the final moment, I have to jump into the sled before it's too late and barrel down the track. Fortunately for me, I have had years of experience running and jumping because of my participation in the long jump. These years of experience gave me a competitive edge over some of the other athletes and helped me with the push start of bobsled.

We practiced at the Ice House in Canada Olympic Park, which was a brand-new first-class track. It's the only place in North America with two ice tracks designed for bobsled and luge and equipped with high-tech equipment to keep the ice in perfect shape for racing. After using the cold, unheated storage area in Park City where the sleds are in boxcar-like metal shipping containers, it felt amazing to use the Ice House storage area for sleds—it is heated.

Having a chance to work out in the facility was a blessing and an advantage for the teams that could come here and train. Typically we get eight to ten rides down the track during the week, which isn't a lot of time for the drivers or the brakewomen to work on their starts. At the Ice House we had a chance to take ten hits or more during a one-hour session. It was a great place to train and I wished that we had a facility like this back in the States.

Bonny was really focused on improving our starts. She wanted to make sure that she was contributing the maximum to our start times, so she took some hits starting at the bar and then she took a few hits from the start block, which allowed her to get a running start. The running start produced faster times. She decided that she would run from the block, so we had to practice hitting the sled at the same time. Over the next few days we practiced this new start several times and felt comfortable with our results. I left Calgary feeling good about our starts and even better about our chances to qualify for the Olympics.

September 11—The World Changes

Once I returned home, I immediately went back to work and resumed my role as a coach. In the afternoons I took advantage of the warm weather by practicing at the local track at Pelham High School. I had complained about the heat as a child, having to practice and roadblock in the heat and humidity for which Alabama is known. But having experienced the extreme cold, I appreciated the southern weather and couldn't imagine living up north where they had a real winter season.

It was a bright sunny day in Birmingham, Alabama, when Johnny left for work. "I love you, baby," is what I said on September 11, 2001, as Johnny left. I had mumbled these words as I rolled over in my bed, hoping for a few more hours of sleep. I loved coming home to my bed, turning the air conditioner down to 65 degrees, bundling up with a lot of covers, with a fan blowing directly on my face. These were my ideal sleeping conditions. I tried to take complete advantage of this opportunity, knowing that I would only be in town a few days.

When I woke up, I started my daily routine by cooking some bacon, eggs, and grits, and I turned on the *Today* show with Katie, Al, and Matt. As I was listening to the TV, I heard that there was breaking news and that's when I found out that the U.S. was under attack. I didn't know what to do. This was the first time I could ever remember us being attacked in the U.S. I called Johnny at work and asked if he heard what was going on. He hadn't, but by the time we had gotten off the phone the word had spread, and for a brief moment it felt like the world was coming to an end. It didn't seem real. How could we be attacked?

I watched TV day and night, curious as to what was going to happen next and wondering if the terrorists would strike again. Johnny called his brother who lived in New York to make sure he wasn't down in the city, and he also contacted other family members to make sure they were okay. I felt helpless, exposed, and violated. I couldn't help but think about the families that lost loved ones and worried about those who were wandering in the streets looking for their family members. It was not a good feeling. I cried several times just looking at the pictures on the TV, and because I realized that I could have been on that plane as easily as someone else. I thanked God for my safety and for my family and friends. I wished that Johnny could have stayed home with me because I felt that I needed his protection. But I knew that the company and his employees needed him at work. I was scared to walk outside, I was terrified of the future, and I feared that the worst was yet to come.

As a part of my life back in Alabama, Johnny and I went to regular services at Faith Chapel Christian Center. After September 11, Pastor Michael Moore, whom we call Pastor Mike, taught a series of messages he called "Fear or Faith." The teaching from these sermons had a powerful effect on my spiritual and emotional health during this trying period.

"Each of us faces the difficulties of life with one of two choices," Pastor Mike explained. "We face them either with fear or with faith. Think about the chair that you are sitting in. Do you have 100 percent confidence the chair is going to hold you?" Everyone in the packed auditorium nodded *yes* in answer to the question. We were following each point with our notebooks open and pens poised to capture notes from Pastor Mike's teaching from the Scriptures.

"There is no in-between," Pastor Mike explained. "All of life is faced with either fear or faith." This simple message was what I needed to give me confidence and restore the faith I had lost after the attacks. I'm sure a lot of people questioned God during this time. Why did He let it happen? Why us? What did we do wrong to deserve this? Everyone had questions and most couldn't provide an answer. Fortunately, Pastor Mike always knew what to say to help us understand what God's will was for our lives. He made it plain and simple—God wanted us to trust in His Word and live each day for Him because we never know when it's going to be our last. The message was clear, but it was tough to digest. There were still so many questions, so many fears, and so many reasons to doubt.

FEAR OR FAITH

Fear or faith? Those simple words continue to ring in my mind. In each situation, we have either faith or fear. It's that simple. I began to analyze every part of my life and before I realized it, I was asking myself this question quite a bit. That's when I recognized many areas where I worried too much, depended on myself, and failed to actually trust God. I kept thinking about Pastor Mike's teaching and it became more and more obvious that I had been depending on my own abilities for quite some time and I really didn't have faith in God. If I really trusted in His words, I wouldn't have to worry so much or try to work things out myself. Those simple words changed my life and I began to realize that I didn't have to live in fear. Pastor Mike encouraged us to go ahead and take our airline flights and carry out our normal routine, but my faith had not overcome my fear of flying since September 11. It would take weeks before I would even consider stepping back on a plane. I had faith that God was going to protect me, but there was no reason to put Him to the test! I figured He would have a better chance of making sure I was safe if I kept my feet on the ground.

At this point in my life bobsled didn't seem that important. I was more concerned about my family and friends. I called Jay and Diane to make sure they were okay, I spoke with Bonny and other members on the team, but I was not ready to get back on a plane and practice bobsled. Fortunately, the coaches were sensitive to the situation and recommended that we cancel the sliding session in Calgary.

My driver, Bonny Warner, took a completely different attitude from mine after the terrorist attacks of September 11. Bonny had taken a leave of absence from her position as a United Airlines captain so she could train for the Olympics. When she found out about the September 11 attacks, she wanted to help in any way that she could and she wanted to encourage people not to be afraid to fly. She called United to volunteer, and spent the next weekend flying six flights out of California, helping reposition airplanes so they could resume their scheduled flights. Since she was not afraid to fly, she decided to head up to Calgary and make use of the start time reserved for the U.S. team.

Immediately people began to fear that the terrorists might be planning an attack at the upcoming Winter Olympic Games. What better way to get the world's attention? Some people recommended that the games be canceled, but others said that if we canceled the games, the terrorists have won. The International Olympic Committee and the Salt Lake Olympic Committee announced that the games would not be canceled. Plans were immediately made to make Salt Lake City the most secure place on earth during the Winter Olympic Games.

There was no question about my desire to go to the Olympics, but I had doubts about our security and whether terrorists would take advantage of having several thousands of people gathered during opening ceremonies. As I began to speculate on the possible areas of attack, I could hear Pastor Mike's voice in my mind saying, "Fear or faith." And with those words I gained the confidence I needed. I refused to stay at home and allow the terrorists to kill my dream.

Some members of the U.S. bobsled team found themselves facing possible military obligations after September 11. Several of them were part of the military WCAP (World Class Athlete Program), among them Jill Bakken, Shauna Rohbock, women's coaches Tuffy Latour and Bill Tavares, and men's bobsled team members Mike Kohn and Doug Sharp. It was a scary situation for those close to the team, and we didn't know what to expect. But the goal of the WCAP is to provide soldiers with world-class potential the opportunity to train in order to compete for a place on the US Olympic Team. These athletes stayed focused on that goal.

TEAM CONTROVERSY

In less than a month I left Birmingham, headed to Park City for our team trials. Johnny was very concerned about me flying. I called him at each of the layovers so that he would not worry as much. I was very cautious and wary of anyone who looked suspicious. I wondered if there were any Federal Air Marshals on the plane and wondered what would happen if our plane was hijacked. I prayed the entire trip and hoped that we arrived safely. I was extremely happy when the plane finally arrived in Salt Lake City, Utah.

Controversy continued to stir among different parts of the women's bobsled team leading up to the October Verizon Championship Series in Park City, Utah. Jill was struggling with some details related to her service in the military. Jean and Jen, who were presented in the media as an inseparable pair and the team to beat, were starting to show some cracks in their partnership. There were rumors that Jean was interested in trying out a new brakewoman named Gea Johnson, a former track athlete and fitness model who had recently begun training for bobsled.

I tried to stay away from the drama because their changes didn't affect our team, and even though I would have liked to push with Jean, I remained loyal to Bonny. Unfortunately, I learned that Bonny also had an interest in trying out Gea. While I chose not to fly after September 11, 2001, I later learned that Bonny had trained at Canada Olympic Park with Gea. This was shocking news to me, because Bonny and I had talked several times and she had never mentioned Gea or the fact that they trained together.

Gea had been training a few days with Jean in Park City, and her start times were very fast. Most thought that Jean might consider changing brakewomen. Instead, she chose to stay with Jen; they would eventually race together in the selection races. Jean and Jen were the best known to the public of all the women's bobsledders—they got a lot of media attention. Their winning streak also meant that everyone expected them to win the gold at the Olympics. Because of this, the stakes were rising higher and higher for every decision Jean Racine made.

While Jean considered switching to Gea, Bonny Warner continued to be very much aware of Gea's performance. Winning races was a key motivating factor for Bonny, and if changing a brakewoman would give her the edge, she was interested. More than anything, Bonny wanted to get on the

Olympic bobsled team. She wondered if I was giving the bobsled a full effort—which I knew I was certainly doing. It was
too bad that Bonny had these types of concerns, which were
unexpressed to me, because it would play into her decisions in
the days ahead. The drama and the switching of the bobsled
teams were just beginning.

The first heat of the Verizon Championship Series began on
a Friday night. The park was closed to the general public; the
only people who could see the race were family members, like
Johnny, and close friends. Even with these restrictions, a large
crowd gathered to cheer and watch the races. Besides the U.S.
men's and women's bobsled teams, there were bobsled athletes
from several other countries. I knew going into these races that
the results would determine our U.S. team rankings as we
headed into the upcoming World Cup series. Three women's
teams had been neck-and-neck, and none of them wanted the
third ranking, because it would put us at a disadvantage in
many ways in the World Cup.

Based on our rankings from the year before, Jean and Jen
raced first and finished with 49.72 seconds. Bonny and I went
second and made it in 50.12 seconds, and Jill and Shauna went
next and ran the course in 49.90. We slipped to third. In the second race, Jean and Jen came in first with 50.01 seconds, Jill and
Shauna in 50.02, and Bonny and I in 50.18. According to the
race rules, each team slides in three heats, and the best two
times are used for the competition. None of us opted for a third
run to improve our standing. Jean was in first place, Jill in second, and Bonny and I in third, but there was one more night of
racing to come.

Saturday evening was especially cold as we prepared to
race. In the first heat, Bonny and I had a remarkable 50.11 run,
which was ahead of Jean's score at 50.18. Jill came in third with
an unexpectedly slow time of 50.51. She had had some bad

news that day from her WCAP commander and was probably not at her best. Then, during the second heat, Jill rallied, and she and Shauna fought their way back into first place with a run of 50.01. Bonny and I stayed in second with a run of 50.23, and Jean followed with 50.24. This night, we all went for the optional third run. In this third heat, Jean performed best with 50.20; Bonny and I slid second with 50.47. Our time turned out to not be enough because Jill drove to a 50.32. When they combined the scores from our four races over two nights, Jill took over USA 1, a position that she had given up in 1998 when Jean Racine joined the team. Jean and Jen were USA 2, and Bonny and I were in the third USA position.

In this highly competitive sport, three teams of extremely close competitors were battling it out for very high stakes. Jean Racine was a great driver, was used to being number one, and was focused on getting it back. Bonny Warner was a very smart athlete with an immense set of skills, and she wanted out of that #3 spot. And the closer we got to the Olympic team trials, the more intense the pressure got.

THE DRIVERS CHANGE
BRAKEWOMEN

Johnny told me, "You need to keep training. God put you in this sport for a reason." I had no idea what would happen, but, in faith, I continued. As I look back, I could never have foreseen what would happen in the days ahead. It was nothing short of remarkable.

Nine
THE DRIVERS CHANGE BRAKEWOMEN

While Jill and Shauna celebrated their top status, Bonny and I were thinking about how to get out of third place. The Olympic trials were just a few months away, and based on these results we wouldn't make the team. There were many questions going through our minds, and none of them would be answered until we mapped out a new game plan. Bonny and I were both disappointed. I felt some pressure, but I knew we had time to get better. The race was close and all we needed was more time to work on our start and more opportunities for Bonny to drive down the track. Bonny was intensely focused on making the improvements it took to win. I knew she was a very driven person and needed to feel that she had done everything possible to do her best, so I didn't worry. This was just her style.

The next day, Sunday, was a day full of photo shoots, radio and television interviews, and press conferences for the three USA teams of women bobsledders. The media were most interested in Jean and Jen, and the USOC officials were clearly promoting them as the top U.S. women's bobsled team and our best chance to win. But the rest of us didn't worry too much about it. We knew that when it all finally shook out, any of us on the women's bobsled team could win the gold medal. Bonny did seem a bit distracted, and Johnny was becoming concerned about her behavior. Gea Johnson had been hanging around, and I got the sense that something was up. But there could have been several reasons for that, and I decided not to worry. Bonny had made such a big deal out of my commitment to the team, and my performances were so strong, that I felt it was best to trust her and work on being a team together.

I did the best I could, smiling for the cameras with Bonny, answering questions, and keeping a positive attitude. I thought it was important and right that we show some team spirit. There was some serious competitive tension in the room, though. It got to the point that some people avoided talking with others unless it was an absolute necessity, but I didn't want to let the competition between us tie me up in knots. To me, it would be very hard to be an Olympian, or to be great at anything, if I allowed my surroundings to cloud my mind with negative thoughts. So I stayed relaxed and tried to have fun talking with the people around me.

THE MEETING

The next night, Bonny Warner asked me, Johnny, the coaches (Bill Tavares, Tuffy Latour, and John Kaus), Olympic team leader Dave Juehring, and Bonny's personal driving coach, Chris Lori, to attend a meeting. Chris Lori did all of the talking. Bonny sat there and listened, along with the rest of us, as he talked about Bonny's goals to make the team. He talked about his expectations and I could tell that he was getting ready to confirm what Johnny and I had felt for the past several days.

As I sat on the floor my blood began to boil. Bonny had been acting weird the past few days. It was obvious from the way Gea Johnson was hanging around and from the nonverbal communication between Bonny and Gea that something was going on. I admit that Bonny and I had different styles of communicating and I knew that this was causing her stress. In the past, some of my teammates and I have been close and others have not. But when it came down to competing, we put our personalities aside. Outside of bobsled, Bonny and I just didn't have a lot in common, but I didn't think that fact would eventually cause our team to self-destruct. Yet as Chris continued talking, he questioned my level of commitment to the sport and my drive to win an Olympic medal. I sat there and listened to this man, knowing that he knew nothing about my desire, my dedication, or my commitment to this sport.

Chris Lori said that he thought it would be a good idea for Bonny to take Gea on tour as her brakewoman for the first half of the season, and let me stay home and rest up for the second half. By this point I knew what they were suggesting but were too afraid to come out and say. Bonny was making moves to replace me with Gea as her partner. I've been involved in many sports, and I had never heard of leaving your #1 athlete at home to let them train. If the athlete is not injured, then she typically gets better as the season progresses. There was only so much that I could do in Birmingham to train for bobsled. I needed to be on tour and on the track with rest of the team.

Under normal circumstances, Johnny is a very laid-back individual and it takes a lot to get him upset. But I could see that he was feeling my rage and did not like what he was hearing. Johnny spoke up for both of us, telling Chris and Bonny, "If you don't take Vonetta to Europe, don't worry about calling her when you return. You need to decide who you want as a brakewoman, because she's not going to wait around for you."

The coaches seemed stunned. They tried to warn Bonny that she was putting her medal chances at risk if she chose Gea over me. They clearly felt that I was the better brakewoman. But it was apparent that Bonny and Chris had already made up their minds; otherwise, I wouldn't have been sitting in that meeting so soon after I helped her qualify for the U.S. national team. The coaches could give advice, but the driver was the one who made the decision about her brakewoman.

It was obvious that the loyalty I had shown Bonny had not been reciprocated. Even though I didn't talk about bobsled every hour of the day, I loved what I was doing and I had committed myself to our team. I wanted her to have the same commitment to us as a team. I was ready for a decision that night that she would be loyal to me. But Bonny stuck with her original plan; she wanted to take Gea to Europe.

After the meeting was over, Johnny and I drove to the house where Bonny was staying and talked with her in great detail about her plan. I wanted to reassure Bonny of my commitment and talk about why this wasn't a good idea for our team. It was clear that she was confused, but she had to make a tough decision. She wanted to win a medal, and I did too, but she felt that because of Gea's fast times that they would make a better team. Emotions ran high and tears were shed, but unfortunately, when Johnny and I left nothing had changed. Our partnership was over. Gea Johnson became Bonny's new brakewoman.

The situation was presented to me as though I was expected to make a choice, but those within the bobsled community know that there are only two seats in the sled and apparently mine had been filled. This conversation ultimately destroyed our team. I wanted to go to the Olympic Games, but my self-respect demanded that I be treated better. My life was full outside of this sport. I was prepared to return to Birmingham and work with the girls on my UAB track team and start my family.

As I look back on what happened, I feel some sympathy for all involved. I think Bonny never expected the situation to become as destructive as it did. She wanted to have a backup brakewoman, with the possibility of moving Gea into my spot. The rules at that time allowed the driver to switch to the brakewoman she thought would be most likely to win. I really just think Bonny did it because of our personality differences. She is very vocal and expressive; I am relaxed and like to make my statements on the track. I think these differences made her uncomfortable. But I do not regret insisting that night that she choose me or Gea.

MOVING ON

After I returned home to Birmingham, I was once again looking at another disappointing end to my Olympic dream. I hated thinking about what happened and couldn't believe that just a few days earlier I was in Salt Lake with Bonny, doing interviews as if we were destined for the Olympics. Now I didn't want to talk about bobsled, I didn't want to watch the Olympics, and I certainly didn't want to end my athletic career like this.

My faith was at an all-time low. Johnny let me deal with the situation internally for a few days and didn't force the issue. But after a few days, he started pushing me to train. Johnny tried to encourage me by saying, "Keep training. I have a feeling someone's going to call you soon." I felt like I had no reason to train. But Johnny kept saying, "God put you in this sport for a reason." Over the next few weeks, Johnny preached to me so much about opportunity and God's plan for my life that I started wondering what it was that God was telling me. Johnny was convinced that either Jean Racine or Jill Bakken would call me. I felt that I was the best brakewoman and would love the opportunity to push with either one of them, but their brakewomen were their best friends, and their relationships seemed to be impenetrable.

At first, I kept training so Johnny would get off my case. Eventually, I started believing in his vision too. During the first week, I was just going through the motions. By the third week, I was starting to get into it and believed that God really did put me in this sport for a reason. To train, I ran a lot, did sprint workouts, and lifted weights.

I hoped that Johnny was right. We began to talk about the possibilities and waited for something positive to happen. Little did I know that my departure was being felt throughout the sport of bobsled. In the next few weeks, I received encouraging e-mails from several folks in the bobsled community. Some of them were aggravated at the way I had been treated, and some just wanted to wish me the best.

In many ways I wanted to give up on the entire sport and quit. Johnny seemed to have much more faith and confidence that another opening would present itself. I've learned that when my faith is weak and Johnny's faith is strong, I can turn and lean on the faith of my husband. It was an important experience for me during those months. I had many doubts and at times wanted to stop training, yet each time that happened, Johnny said, "No, you need to keep training and keep working out. God put you in this sport for reason." I had no idea what would happen, but, in faith, I continued working on my sport. As I look back, I could have never foreseen what would happen in the days ahead. It was nothing short of remarkable.

WORLD CUP SEASON

The women's World Cup bobsled season began without me in November 2001. There were to be eight World Cup races on four different tracks in November and December, and they would all be run before the U.S. Olympic trials were held on December 21. The World Cup races were important, but in this situation they were almost like precursors to the U.S. Olympic trials. The three top U.S. women drivers would compete against each other all season until the trials, when one of them was going to be cut. Each of the U.S. women's bobsled drivers wanted to win the first Olympic gold medal ever for their sport. And they wanted their performance in the World Cup season to show them a smooth path to the top spot.

Of course, the dominant competitors from other countries would be in the World Cup races as well. Susi-Lisa Erdmann and Sandra Prokoff of Germany would be there, as would Francoise Burdet of Switzerland. But the women of the U.S. seemed distracted by the competition for the two places on the U.S. Olympic team, and were almost competing more against each other than against other nations.

Using the Internet, I followed the various race results back home in Birmingham. For the first six races of the season, the U.S. women drivers turned in wildly inconsistent performances. Races one and two were at Winterberg, Germany. Sandra Prokoff, Susi Erdmann, and Francoise Burdet placed 1-2-3 in both races, reminding the U.S. drivers that there's a big world out there. In race one, Jean and Jen were fourth, Bonny and Gea came in fifth, and Jill and Shauna were sixth. In race two, Bonny came fourth, Jean was fifth, and Jill dropped to eighth. In race three at Königssee, Germany, Bonny and Jean moved up a notch to third and fourth, and Jill stayed in eighth.

In race four, Jean, Bonny, and Jill were 2-3-4. Jean, who had medaled in all her races of the previous two seasons, was in a new position for her experience. She had been winning since she switched to bobsled from luge five years earlier. Bonny and Gea, however, seemed to be gelling as a team and were giving Jean and Jen a real run for their money. Jill was having continuing problems with her military obligations, and that created stress for her during the first part of the season. In race four at Igls, Jean and Jen came in third, Jill and Shauna in sixth, and Bonny and Gea in ninth. In race six, Bonny came in fourth, Jill in seventh, and Jean in eleventh place. Things were not evening out, and the drivers and coaches took stock.

MY PHONE RINGS

During the last part of November, Johnny's prediction came true. I got a call from Jean Racine, asking if I would travel with her team and alternate races with Jen for the remainder of the season. Then she would decide just before the Olympics who would race with her for the medal. I wasn't fond of the idea of sharing time, so I told her that I would think about it and let her know something soon. Jean and Jen were such good friends that I knew this was hard for Jean. But she knew that she had to make some changes quickly because Bonny was rising in the rankings.

A few days later, though, Johnny's second prediction came true. Jill Bakken called and asked if I would do a push-off with Shauna. Jill was willing to go with the best pusher right then, race the rest of the World Cup season with her, and take her to the Olympics. It turns out that the coaches had been urging Jill for some time to consider another brakewoman, but she had wanted to stick with Shauna. After the sixth race of the World Cup season, the coaches asked her again. Jill talked to Shauna, who was upset at first, but then agreed to the push-off with me. Shauna was a real class act about the whole thing. She was a loyal friend to Jill even during this difficult situation. And Jill went out of her way to let Shauna know that she valued her friendship.

I began to think that God did have a plan for my life and that He wanted to somehow use me in this sport. It was a huge turnaround from a couple of weeks earlier, when I was ready to quit. I was glad that I chose to release my faith and continue training; otherwise, I wouldn't have been ready to accept these opportunities. I felt strong and rested and ready to face the challenge. I knew that it was tough for both Jean and Jill to call me, given the fact they were sliding with their best friends. Deep down, both realized that they would need the fastest brakewoman in their sled in order to have a chance at the Olympic trials.

This was a true test for me. Johnny and I discussed both options, and felt that going full speed in one direction is better than going half speed in two directions. I work better having a clear picture of what's going on. I think most athletes would agree that it creates a better environment for training and competing when the rules are clear. So I thanked Jean for the offer and told her that I would not be joining Jen as an alternate. I felt that I had proven myself and I wasn't interested in splitting time with anyone.

After I made my decision, I spoke with the coaches and with Jill to let them know of my intentions. I had prayerfully considered pushing with Jean, but that little voice kept telling me to go with Jill. This was not the popular decision, and I often wonder what others on the team would have done if given the choice, but I had to do what I believed was right for me even if that meant that we didn't win a medal. I would leave Birmingham with a clear plan and a focus.

THE PUSH-OFF AND THE SWITCH-OFF

The push-off took place during the training week in Calgary before the last two World Cup races. Others like Gea and Bethany decided to push that day as well, but the competition was between Shauna and me. After our three runs, it was clear that my times were faster than Shauna's. It looked as if Jill would ask me to become her brakewoman. It was also clear that Gea was a fast brakewoman as well. We tied on our first two pushes and she edged me out by .02 seconds on our final push.

In the next couple of days, I learned that after our push competition, Jean Racine asked Gea Johnson to become her new brakewoman. Gea had hesitated at first, then agreed. This left Bonny Warner out in the cold. Because the press was so aware of Jean and Jen as a longstanding team, it was a big deal in the media when Jean made the switch. Jean was painted as a betrayer, a disloyal friend. Jen went public with her accusations against Jean. The media had a field day with it. Their friendship was destroyed after that.

It's hard to understand the situation from outside. The relationship between a bobsled driver and a brakewoman is a complicated mix of friendship and sportsmanship, loyalty and competition. It's true for the men's teams, too. We were all athletes who wanted to do our best, make it to the Olympics, and win. We were also on a team, and needed our partner to be the very best in order to win. We all had our own traits that played into the process—my quiet personality mixed with Bonny's driven nature led to one switch. Jean and Jen's friendship started out giving them a strong advantage and then that intensity turned negative. Jill and Shauna maintained their friendship, but there was less public pressure on them than on Jean and Jen. And all this happened in a pressure cooker of a situation—the first-ever Olympic women's bobsled year. I feel compassion for all involved when I look back on the drama we went through.

My friends and family who watched the process may wonder why I hung in there. I am an athlete. I wanted to compete. I continued to cling to my quiet faith in God throughout the changing process. I trusted God to use my training and my efforts and to control my steps. Johnny and I prayed throughout the entire process about my involvement in bobsled and whether it should continue. During the two-month period when I was at home in Birmingham, my faith and trust in God was my sustaining power. In the whirlwind of changing partners, I continually tried to listen to the still, small voice of God. I remained consistent in reading my Bible and turning to it for strength and also in prayer. The lessons would help me in the days ahead.

As we moved toward the Olympic trials, the teams were redefined. I was teamed with Jill Bakken, Jean Racine had Gea Johnson as her brakewoman, and Bonny Warner was sliding with Jen Davidson (Jean's former partner). Jill and I began practicing together, and Shauna Rohbock was always present and helping our efforts. Naturally, she felt disappointed that she wasn't going to the Olympic Games, but she was determined to continue supporting her friend Jill. Her attitude made a huge impression on everyone.

THE BAKKEN-FLOWERS TEAM

Jill and I had our first race together in World Cup race seven in Calgary on December 15, 2001. I remember being very excited because this was the same track where the movie *Cool Runnings* was filmed. None of the other teams or the U.S. coaches knew what to expect from us. Jill and I had only been practicing together for two days. Fortunately, it didn't take a long time for us to click. Jill and I have similar personalities—Bonny had actually commented before on how much alike Jill and I are, and she was right in the sense that we are both shy and a little unassuming. I like to make my statements on the track versus talking about what I can do.

We broke the start record in our first race together. We had the fastest start times of all the sliders and we set a new start record at 5.74. Even though we finished fifth, I realized that Jill and I could produce amazing results as a team. I was very excited and optimistic about our possibility of being the number one U.S. team headed into the Olympics. With our push times and Jill's experience on the track, there was no reason why we couldn't beat anyone on the track in Salt Lake.

Our old friends from Germany and Switzerland were in top

form again. In race seven, Susi Erdmann took first, Francoise Burdet took second, and Sandra Prokoff took third. Jean and Gea did well, placing fourth, almost a tenth of a second ahead of Jill and me in fifth. Bonny and Jen placed seventh. We were all getting used to new partners and learning to work together.

Sunday was the final race of the 2001–2002 World Cup season. With each heat, Jill's level of confidence was rising and nothing could dampen it. It continued even when Germans Prokoff and Holzner beat the start record we had set the day before by two one-hundredths of a second (5.72). Our overall time was not great, and we placed fifth in that race. Jean and Gea took the silver medal with this race, and Bonny, racing with Bethany Hart, slid to seventh.

Whatever else happened as a result of the partner switching, Jean Racine had taken the wind out of Bonny Warner's sails. Bonny would have a hard time recovering. Jill and I felt it was obvious that we could push fast together. We looked forward to returning to the Park City track, which Jill knew particularly well.

Reaching for the Olympics

The last World Cup race was on Sunday, December 16, and the Olympic trials would begin just five days later in Park City. I headed back with Jill to Park City to prepare. There would be two heats each day on Friday and Saturday, and the top two teams would be determined. Soon the big question would be answered—who would go to the Olympics?

During the days before the trials, each of us tried to solidify our new relationships with our partners. We tried to avoid the media circus, which was easier for some of us than others. Jean Racine, Jen Davidson, and Gea Johnson faced an onslaught from the press, who clamored for the inside scoop. Bonny also did her best to avoid the clamor, to focus and prepare for the trials.

In my steady, easygoing way, I was preparing myself, getting my mind and body ready to do my very best. We would see what happened. I was excited to have a shot at getting on an Olympic team and I was praying and trusting these trials would have a much stronger result for me than the Sacramento trials had. In my heart, I knew that only God had the ability to see my future.

THE OLYMPIC TRIALS

I stood there in the snow in disbelief; this little girl from Birmingham, Alabama, had made the Winter Olympic team, and it just didn't seem real. I began to realize that God wasn't fooling when He planted that Olympic dream in me as a child. He really did have a plan for my life.

Ten
THE OLYMPIC TRIALS

As we arrived in Park City to begin preparing for the Olympic trials, different members of the team were still trying to understand the last-minute changes of the World Cup. I was excited to participate with Jill in the trials and my focus was on our team and our success during the next couple of weeks. When I talked with Jill, I could tell that she was prepared and full of self-assurance. Because she knew the track at Park City so well, she felt great about our chances there. I knew that, based on our results in Calgary, we could push just as fast, if not faster, than any other team on tour. This was our home track and we wanted a chance to show the other U.S. teams, and the world, what we could do. At the same time, I think Jill still felt a little bad about making the switch to me from Shauna. Shauna was her best friend, and she wanted to stick with her, but it would have meant risking her chance to represent her country in the Olympics. Therefore, she made the tough choice and put her feelings aside in hopes of securing a spot on the Olympic team. Shauna helped, though, by being completely supportive of Jill, showing up for practices, and encouraging her to stay calm and do her best. Jill would often get nervous before races, and Shauna knew this. She didn't want to undercut her friend, and she did everything she could to help Jill feel confident. She was terrific. We were also very glad that the press was leaving us alone.

Bonny announced that she had selected Bethany Hart as her brakewoman. This left Jen Davidson out of a job and out in the cold. According to Bonny, she and Bethany worked well together and their starts were constantly improving. The drivers simply wanted the fastest push they could get. The media was pressing Jean Racine to talk more about her change of brakewomen to Gea Johnson, but she answered with silence. Instead, Jean focused on the race. Gea's push times were good, and Jean felt she had made the right decision to switch partners. But the partner switches on the U.S. team didn't make sense to the public. Many people don't understand that almost all of the decisions about brakewomen were related to concrete, measurable push times. Also, we were very concerned that at the Olympic Games we would be facing our rival German and Swiss teams, who had been dominating the World Cup races that year. We needed every advantage.

Each sled now had a new combination for the Olympic trials. The team members put aside these "extra" distractions and instead focused on our work ahead—sliding on the Olympic track. The Olympic trials and the Olympic competition itself would be held on the Park City track. This track had a shorter push area, and therefore required the push athletes to deliver an explosive burst of speed at the start—not a gradual buildup. The drivers focused on giving every bit of strength they could during the shorter time they pushed. Then their job was to deliver a smooth, fearless ride down the track, letting the sled pick up as much speed as possible on the turns and avoiding bumps, skids, and, worst of all, crashes. Each of the newly formed teams spent the week on these goals. All three teams now had the superior Bo-Dyn sleds, so no one was at a disadvantage with equipment.

Our coaches and trainers understood the importance of getting into a rhythm and familiar pattern for our workouts. Our

practice sessions were designed to match the race day so everything would feel familiar when the race was on the line. These
practice sessions helped us get accustomed to the sled work
that had to be done prior to sliding—lifting weights, eating,
and finding the time to rest in between. Our start times and finish times, in practice, are always slower than race times, but
based on the practice times we can get a feel of how fast our
starts are going to be and how fast our overall or down time
will be on race day. Each day I began to feel better about our
chances based on the results from practice. Jill and I began to
gel as a team, and our times were reflective of our willingness
to train hard each day. Neither of us did a lot of talking—Jill
knew what she had to do in terms of driving and I understood
my role as brakewoman. I was very happy to be with a driver
who truly appreciated my abilities to help the team.

JOHNNY ARRIVES

Johnny arrived in Salt Lake a couple of days before the
Olympic trials. He joined me at Jay and Diane Maynard's house
for the biggest week of my life. He understood exactly what I
had been going through and was happy to see me "live out his
bobsled dream." I felt more comfortable with him being there.
I knew deep down that he had been pushing me to do this
because he wanted to see me fulfill my own dreams. I had
waited for this day all my life and I felt my confidence growing. I had always been an underdog at the trials, but this time
felt different.

The day before the women's bobsled trials, Johnny and I
went to see the speed skating trials. We had never seen a speed
skating event on TV or in person, and we thought it would be
a good opportunity to see some of the athletes who would represent the U.S. I was particularly interested in seeing Apolo
Ohno. The media loved Apolo, and I was curious to see him in

person because I probably wouldn't have a chance once the Games started. He had become one of the big stories prior to the Olympics, and I wanted to see the guy who had a chance to win at least four gold medals. The trip gave me an opportunity to relax and see other athletes fighting for a spot to make the Olympics. It also gave me some perspective. The Olympics are full of stories, dramas, and close competitions—we weren't the only ones. So few people actually make the Olympics, and there are so many people who try.

After the event, we drove back to Park City for a meeting of the men's and women's bobsled teams. Every person officially involved in bobsled was required to be at this important session: athletes, coaches, and a few designated Olympic officials. Our Olympic team leader, Dave Juehring, encouraged us to do our best, and let us know about some of the rules for the Olympic team, which would be created from tomorrow's competition. There would be two women's bobsled teams, USA 1 and USA 2. There would be no alternates. In the past, alternates had traveled with the team—Bethany Hart had done an awesome job as alternate in the previous World Cup season and had been desperately needed for that.

Dave Juehring also addressed the recent brake-switching frenzy (the men's team had had their own series of switches going on at the same time as ours, although the press was more interested in the women's teams). He told us that he was going to ask every driver to name a brakeman or brakewoman right then, and that brakeperson would be the driver's partner for the trials and for the Olympics. No switching from then on. An athlete would only be replaced if they were incapacitated by injury. Then he asked the drivers to name their brakewomen. Bonny named Bethany Hart, Jean named Gea, and Jill named me. These were the only three U.S. women's bobsled teams with enough World Cup points to go to the Olympics. There were two other teams who would be competing in the trials the next day—the Donna McAleer-Shannon Hartnett team, and Margery Holman and Carol Lewis, sister of Olympic runner Carl Lewis. This second group just wanted to compete and see how they stacked up against the field. On each of the two race days, every team would have three runs down the track, and their best two times would count toward the results.

After the meeting we went our separate ways and focused on our race. Johnny and I enjoyed dinner with Jay, Diane, and Shannon. Diane had prepared one of Johnny's favorite dishes, spaghetti and meatballs. Johnny loved Diane's special recipe, and I loved her pot roast. We talked and laughed for hours. Before we knew it, it had gotten late, but Johnny still insisted on getting me ready for the reporters. So he pulled out our camcorder and began asking me a series of questions. He filmed me as I wrapped my hair and brushed my teeth and expected me to play along with his Q&A session. I kept telling him, "Don't film me!" but he wanted to capture my emotions the night before our big race. The round of questions went on for about 15 minutes before he decided that he had enough footage for his home videos. I quickly turned the lights off, we said a prayer, and I tried to get some rest.

THE OLYMPIC TRIALS

Friday, December 21, 2001, began with optimism, hope, and a prayer. Johnny grabbed my hands and began praying:

> On this day we give thanks for this opportunity
> and are grateful to be in this position.
> We believe that You have not brought us this far
> for failure.
> Your plan is to have us achieve greatness in this
> sport, and through praise and worship

we thank You in advance for Your guidance
and for Your hand of mercy
and for Your discipline
and for our pastor Michael Moore.
We are operating in faith,
Amen.

Jill and I prepared for the race, polishing our runners and look-ing over every piece of equipment to check and double-check it before the race. As Friday evening came, it was getting close to race time. Because there was a massive amount of construction in progress to prepare for the Olympic Games, the trials were closed to the general public. Nevertheless, a crowd of a few hundred people made up of family and friends managed to get into the park. They were wrapped up warm to endure the time standing in the snow and freezing weather.

Jill and I joked as we warmed up together. We had very similar personalities in that we always seemed very relaxed, even before the biggest race of our life. As I ran, I thought about my childhood days in Alabama and couldn't believe that I had been given one more chance to qualify for the Olympics. I said a quick prayer for our team and thanked God for bringing me to this point. I knew that I belonged here, and that He had allowed those other things to happen so that I would under-stand how amazing He is. It was wonderful to be facing the biggest challenge of my life in a spirit of praise at God's good-ness.

I watched Jill slip into a quiet spot near the start house to get ready. She was feeling her usual nervousness, and was fighting it by focusing and calming herself. She imagined her-self driving down the track, and with her eyes closed, she held her hands like she was steering the sled through every piece of the perfect run. She was the only member of the original U.S.

women's bobsled team who was still competing, and her years of experience and dedication were rising to the front.

Finally, the race officials called for the trials to officially begin. For the first heat of the day, Bonny-Bethany drew the first run, Jean-Gea the second, and Jill and I the third. After the forerunners slid down the track to check the timing eyes and make certain the ice was ready for the race, the serious racing started. Bonny and Bethany had a start time of 5.48 and drove to a 50.23 finish. The second team, Jean and Gea, improved to a 5.37 start time with a final of 49.66. Jill and I exactly matched Jean and Gea's start time of 5.37, but our final was one tiny hundredth of a second slower, at 49.67.

We loaded our sleds into the back of the truck and began to drive back up the mountain for our second run. I looked at Jill and smiled. Without saying anything, she and I both knew what it meant. We would probably make the first U.S. women's Olympic bobsled team. We had a chance to be a part of history. I was so thankful that God presented this opportunity and that I had accepted the challenge. I knew that it had been a rough and rocky road, but God had given me the strength to endure.

For the second heat of the evening, the worst time of the previous three went first. Bonny and Bethany's start time slipped to 5.52, and they had a problem on one of the curves. They crossed the line at 50.13 seconds, which meant their combined time was 1:40.36 for the two heats.

Next it was our turn for a second run. Jill and I hit the sled with a pretty good 5.39 start. As Jill drove down the track and I rode with my head tucked between my knees, I could tell we were hitting greater speeds than we had before—I later found out our top speed was 81.92 miles per hour. We crossed the finish at 49.89 seconds, and our combined time for both heats was 1:39.56. Next, the final team pushed off for their second heat. Jean and Gea had a 5.40 push, and Jean drove to a top speed of

82.27 miles per hour. For the heat, the pair clocked in at 49.55 seconds and maintained their first place position with a combined score for the night of 1:39.21. Everyone decided not to take the optional third run.

After the race, Jill and I felt great—confident and happy. I kept hugging Johnny and rejoicing at the results after this first day of the trials. I knew Saturday night would be the final push, but I also knew our team and Jean's were significantly ahead, and close to securing our places on the Olympic team. It was hard to control my emotions. My heart was still in race mode. I would have liked for us to finish in first, but at this point I was very happy being second. All we needed to do was have two more good runs and we would be on our way to the Olympics. I knew that I had to calm down in order to get some rest, but I could hardly sleep. I wanted to race again. I wanted it to be over and I wanted to be on the team.

The next evening the crowds of family and friends were back for the second and final day of the trials. First down the track, Bonny and Bethany gave a huge push and achieved a 5.49 start (it was their personal best for the trials) and clocked a time of 49.50 seconds. Next, Jill and I had a 5.37 push and finished with 49.05 seconds. Finally, Jean and Gea started with 5.39 seconds and then Jean aggressively drove to a new course record of 48.92. She is a phenomenally talented driver. We were all pushing each other to some of the fastest times ever driven on that track.

I wanted to scream! My chances of going to the Olympics were real. I knew that all we had to do was take one more trip and I would be an Olympian...*we* would be Olympians. I couldn't wait for our last run. Jill and I kept smiling at each other while trying to stay focused. I knew that Jill could have driven this track with one eye closed. Jill told me that her eyesight is so bad that it probably wouldn't make a difference anyway if her eyes were open or closed. I liked to think that they were always open! I understood that she was so confident and comfortable that it was almost like putting the sled on autopilot. She had driven down this track so many times, but none was more important than our last run.

We prepared for the last race of the day. For their final start, Bonny and Bethany clocked 5.65 seconds with a track time of 49.93. Next, Jill and I went. We pushed for a quick 5.39 start. As the G-forces picked up inside the sled, I could feel that we were topping our previous day's speeds (our top speed for this run turned out to be 83.1 miles per hour). I thought we might even beat Jean and Gea this time, but we had a little trouble as we headed into curve 15. We skidded briefly and hit the side once, and it slowed our run slightly to a 49.26-second final. Jean and Gea managed a 5.45 start and clocked a 49.25-second run. Bonny decided against a third run down the track and her decision finalized the two teams that were going to the Olympics—and I was in one of those two teams!

I immediately started crying. It didn't seem real. Several emotions quickly surged through my body. The cold was no longer a factor. I felt like I was floating on air because my feet didn't touch the ground. I ran across the ice to congratulate everyone that was there. My stomach was turning, my mind was still trying to process what just happened, and my skin was tingling with excitement. I hugged everybody on the team, starting with Jill and ending with Matt Roy, the executive director. I cried on coach Bill Tavares's shoulder and thanked him for all that he did. Then I grabbed Johnny, held him close, and told him how much I loved him and appreciated him, and then we both starting crying. But it wasn't until I looked over and saw Jay Maynard wipe tears from his eyes that I realized that our victory was bigger than Jill and me.

Our victory meant that everyone whom we were connected

to also made the Olympic team. All of those people had taken the run down the track with us and they were as excited as we were. Jay and Diane had been supportive, but I had no idea how much it meant to them for us to qualify for the team. I looked at Jay and I ran over and hugged him and thanked him for all of his support. It really did something to me to see him show his emotions. I'm very emotional and I like to see others express themselves the way I do. But it is rare to see a man show his emotions. I knew that he must have really understood how I was feeling. Seeing him cry made me appreciate everything that I had been through, and seeing us win made him appreciate all that they had been through. They sacrificed their time and welcomed us into their family, and now all of us were going to the Olympics. My heart was pounding, my eyes were full of tears, and I felt like everything that happened this night was a replay of my childhood dream. I dreamed of making the team many times, but each time when I woke, I discovered that it was only a dream. Part of me was still in shock and unsure if I was dreaming and the other part didn't want to wake up and find out.

I stood there in the snow in disbelief; this little girl from Birmingham, Alabama, had made the Winter Olympic team, and it just didn't seem real. I began to realize that God wasn't fooling when He planted that Olympic dream in me as a child. He really did have a plan for my life. He had been constantly preparing me for this opportunity and I was happy that I had had faith even when it seemed foolish to do so. Just three weeks ago I was in Birmingham hoping that someone would call me, and now I was here. God saw past the few days that I spent at home without a team; He saw my future and in it was victory.

While I was celebrating my place on the U.S. Olympic team, some of the other sliders were watching their dreams come to an end. I'm especially thinking of Bonny Warner, who brought me into the sport of bobsled. For this I will always be grateful to her. She had poured so much energy into getting on the team, and now it was apparent that she didn't make it. Jay and Diane cared very much for Bonny, and I think that mixed in Jay's tears of happiness for me were also tears of sadness for Bonny. Bonny was 39 years old, and this was probably her last Olympic attempt.

Over at the end of the track, the four of us who were headed to the Olympics—Jean, Gea, Jill, and me—met with the press briefly to talk about becoming America's Olympic bobsled teams, then we went for our mandatory drug testing. The drug testing procedure was standard after the races, and random drug testing could happen any time and any place. It comes with the territory of athletics.

Later that night, we went to Jay and Diane's and celebrated with everybody in the community. I smiled so much that my cheeks started hurting. This was a unique experience for everyone who had supported us from the beginning. They had listened to my bobsled stories and had watched me grow from a person who knew nothing about bobsled to a person who would ultimately represent the U.S. in the Olympics. Next to marrying Johnny, this was no doubt the happiest day of my life!

Around 2:00 A.M. we decided that it was time to get some rest. Before going to sleep, I sat on the side of the bed and read some letters from the students at Greystone Elementary School in Birmingham, Alabama. Barry Evans's wife, Jeri, worked for Greystone Elementary School and she asked her students to write me letters. Barry was a manager who worked with Johnny at Blue Cross and Blue Shield of Alabama. Each night I would read the letters and use them to motivate me to do my best. I appreciated all the time and effort that went into their drawings and poems. I loved getting this fan mail and I wanted to make them proud. A few minutes later I laid down. I don't think I ever went to sleep; I remember repeating this phrase over and over..."I'm going to the Olympics...I'm going to the Olympics...I'm going to the Olympics."

After the trials, everyone went home for the Christmas and New Year's holidays. Johnny and I returned to Birmingham. We joined our immediate family and our church family at Faith Chapel. In many ways, during those few days of being home, I was glad to return to a normal life—to slip into the movies or spend time with my family or simply enjoy being with Johnny. I continued working out and training, but it was a complete change of pace for me. Also during this time, I checked in with the UAB track team, where I had kept my position as an assistant coach. It was great to see my girls! I wanted them to know that I was there for them—that I was interested in how they were doing and that they could call me when they needed to. They were more interested in my story—that I was going to the Olympics. It was a time of excitement for all of us.

After I made the Olympic team, the city of Birmingham got more interested in the sport of bobsled. The local paper started a series following my Olympic journey. Traffic to my Web site picked up significantly. People e-mailed me to wish me well—it was terrific! But even with this new attention, I still found the time at home to be relaxing. It was so much easier than the pressure-filled competitive situations I had been in for the last few months.

While Johnny and I were relaxing in Birmingham and getting mentally prepared for the Olympic Games in February, some of the fallout of the partner switching was being aired in the press. Jen Davidson, Jean Racine's former partner, filed a grievance with the U.S. Bobsled and Skeleton Federation asserting that she was unfairly denied her Olympic chances and demanding that she be given a race-off for an Olympic spot. The press picked up on this and started calling Jean

"Mean Jean Racine" and highlighting the drama of Jean and Jen and Gea's partner switch. Jean defended her decision, but this period of time was really hard for her.

The press didn't make a big deal out of Bonny's and my breakup, probably because it had happened months earlier and Bonny was no longer a contender. Bonny was also interested in moving on—she had been asked by NBC to return to her job as Olympic commentator for these games. Jill and Shauna's situation was handled with such goodwill between them that it was hardly remembered. Their friendship was strong again and Shauna was turning her attention to her future in the sport. Occasionally an article would mention our partner switches, mainly to make the point that "this is how it is" in the sport of bobsled. But mostly we were left alone.

The attention was relentless for Jean's team, though. Early on, Jean had sought media attention by getting an agent. Because there's a small window of opportunity, an agent can help make connections that are beneficial for an athlete's success. But unfortunately this situation was gaining speed in the wrong direction. Only time could change everyone's perception of Jean. Some people also felt that the situation received attention because the competitors were women—no one would criticize a man for going with the faster partner over a friend.

Unfortunately, this media frenzy was not good for women's bobsled. We needed to be focusing on our sport instead of defending it. This matter could only take our focus off of training for the Olympics. Ultimately, Jen Davidson's complaint failed. The USBSF decided that the teams that qualified at the trials would be the teams to represent the U.S. at the Olympics.

On January 16th we left Salt Lake City to train at the Olympic Training Center in Chula Vista, California. All of us were scheduled to be there training for two weeks. Johnny managed to come out and help me train, and I couldn't have been happier. I looked forward to it as a change of pace from the work on the ice and a chance to work on our speed training and weight lifting.

Even though we were a long way from our bobsleds, Jill and I still practiced our timing. Whether we had ice or not, we stood back to back and went through the start triggers.

"Back set," I called.

"Front set. Ready. GO!" Jill called. Then together we clapped and turned. We repeated this exercise until we were in perfect synchronization.

Being in California also gave us a chance to just train and not worry about any of the other distractions. Jill and I had been asked for several interviews after the trials, but most of the attention was focused on Jean. Jean and Gea were still favored to win as we headed into the Olympics, but Jill and I didn't mind. We liked not having the extra attention on us. We used this time in California to become more unified and better acquainted. I was happy to get back to warmer weather and back on the track.

Because we were so much in the background to the public eye, we were officially named "the other team" by our teammates and coaches. It was all in fun, but we realized that no one really knew a lot about us. We didn't seek attention and we were not concerned about the media hype. We were there to medal. All of the other things that come with participating in the Olympics were a bonus. We often talked about how the media would go into frenzy if we shocked the world and won instead of the other teams picked to medal. The story would read: "And out of nowhere the other U.S. team wins the gold... and who are they again?" It didn't bother either one of us to be in the background and away from the spotlight of the media. We were underdogs, and deservedly so; we had only raced two times together and in both races we shocked the field.

After we came back from San Diego, Jill and I both came down with a stomach virus, but we didn't let that slow us down. During the first week of February, we were sliding in Park City and it was important to get that time on the ice. It marked our only time to practice until February 16, which was three days before the Olympic race. "The other team" was going to give it their all.

THE LONGEST 17 DAYS OF MY LIFE

As I walked into the stadium with the other athletes, I could hear the crowd roaring, "USA! USA!" For years, I had watched these ceremonies on television, and now I was one of the people representing my country.

Eleven
THE LONGEST 17 DAYS OF MY LIFE

On February 2, 2002, I was invited to a Park City art museum to help the kids celebrate their artwork. Chevy and the "Team Behind the Team" organizers asked if I would come and be a part of this ceremony. I was honored that I had this opportunity, and excited that I had a chance to sign some autographs. This was the first time I signed autographs as an Olympian. I was an Olympian! There was so much going on during the next few weeks, and I wanted to have fun, but I was so anxious that I began to look at my watch constantly, which made the time go even slower. Being there made me realize how good it felt to finally achieve my goal. It was nice to have a chance to take pictures and be a part of the event. It really meant a lot for me to be able to allow others to share my Olympic experience. I left there hoping that I could one day inspire the youth of America just as Jackie Joyner-Kersee had inspired me for so many years.

General Motors (Chevy "Team Behind the Team") had also submitted my name to take part in the Olympic Torch Relay. I had always dreamed of carrying the torch and had practiced several times in front of the mirror. I knew exactly how I would run, smile, and wave to the crowd. My only concern was making sure that I didn't trip and cause the flame to go out. I didn't want to receive my 15 minutes of fame on the bloopers reel.

Jay and Diane Maynard gave me some pointers about the

Torch Relay. Jay had carried the torch a few days earlier in California and was still excited about his experience. Because Jay had purchased his torch after he carried it, I was able to get a feel for how heavy it was. While I jogged in place in their living room, I waved to the crowd and smiled as if I was actually running in the relay. Diane warned me to be patient. She said that I needed to run slowly. She knew this because Jay had taken off once the torch was passed to him. He was so caught up in the moment that he didn't take time to enjoy it. It was more like a sprint than a casual jog. I wish I could have been there. Jay's excitement hadn't ended. He designed a wooden torch holder that included a place to insert a picture, and made one for each of us. So many of my dreams were coming true, and I knew that I would remember these experiences for a lifetime.

Two days later I drove down to Salt Lake to pick up Johnny from the airport. He had flown in to help me train and watch me carry the torch. On February 5, we drove a little more than 2 hours to a little town called Ephraim, Utah. I had never heard of Ephraim, but I was excited to be there. We ate burgers and drank strawberry shakes in preparation for my Olympic Torch debut. It probably wasn't the most nutritious meal, but it tasted so good!

At 2:20 the torch carriers were scheduled to be at the meeting place for processing. Media and newspaper reporters were all around, but the focus wasn't on me. Until the very end, no one in the media knew I was there. Everyone was taking pictures and talking with a man from the community, who was carrying the torch on the same day he celebrated his 100th birthday. He was great! I looked at him as he ran/walked with the torch and thought, *I hope I'm in as good a shape as he's in when I'm his age.* He deserved the attention. Before I left, I made sure I took a picture with him. It was inspiring to see him take part in the relay and it really signified what the Olympics were all about. The Games are truly special and it brings people from all ages together to celebrate the spirit of the Olympics.

During processing, I learned that I would receive the torch around 4:07. I was anxious and ready to feel the electricity of the crowd and be part of this ceremony. The Olympic Flame had not been in the United States since the 1996 Summer Games in Atlanta. Before the Winter 2002 Olympics began, it had traveled through 46 states, with 11,500 people cooperating to pass along the three-pound torch.

All of us who were carrying the torch rode a bus to our start point and waited for our turn. I was selected to be the last person to carry the torch, carry it on stage, and light the cauldron. The selection added just a little more pressure to my experience. I felt so patriotic. I waited my turn and smiled and talked to people as they exited the bus to wait for their turn. Finally it was my turn. I remember my heart beating fast as I ran down the sidewalk and onto the stage. It seemed as if everyone in Ephraim was screaming and chanting. I knew they were not screaming for me, but for what I was carrying and representing—the Olympic Torch. It was truly amazing!

I considered it a privilege to join the other Americans who had carried the torch in preparation for the beginning of the Winter Olympics. This experience was remarkable. Once it was over, I was even closer to the date when Jill and I would compete. From my perspective, the day of our competition couldn't get here fast enough.

THE OLYMPIC VILLAGE

I could feel the buzz and excitement in the air. The date was February 7, 2002, and Jill and I joined athletes from around the world as we settled into our dorm rooms on the University of Utah campus. As everyone had promised after September 11, the security for the Olympics was very tight, and we felt secure once we made it pass the multiple guards and checkpoints. The U.S. team had an entire dorm. Some of the smaller countries had to share, but we needed the space due to the sheer number of athletes that were representing the U.S.

Along with living quarters, the Olympic Village featured gift shops, coffeehouses, a game room, a place to watch movies, and several restaurants. McDonald's was the premier restaurant in the village, and I couldn't wait to find out if they had the crispy apple pies. Even though I don't eat the apples, I love the crust and the filling. The restaurants stayed open 24 hours a day and they were always filled with people, regardless of what time I went in there. There were also trainers available, a sitting area, and a spot to watch TV. They offered manicures and pedicures. I wanted to do it all, because this was truly a once-in-a-lifetime opportunity. I wanted to make sure I fully enjoyed every minute of it.

There was always something going on at the Village. On the night that we moved in we learned that Coolio would be performing. I was familiar with his music and intrigued by his personality. Jill and I thought it would be a great way to relax a little before the Opening Ceremony. We were right. Coolio was all over the place, dancing, singing, and having fun. Before the night was done, all of the girls and some of the guys from the bobsled team were on stage with Coolio learning some new moves.

THE OPENING CEREMONY

The day had finally arrived! February 8th marked the beginning of the Olympics. Jill and I had our separate journeys that brought us to the Olympics, but now we were teammates and roommates. Our goal had never been clearer, nor had it been so close—we could almost reach it. We kept each other laughing and tried to stay relaxed, because we knew what was at stake. Whenever our adrenaline started pumping and the anticipation was too much to bear, we'd joke with each other by saying, "Grab your helmet and your shoes if you're ready to race."

Jill and I were ready to race, but we also were excited about taking part in the Opening Ceremony. Before it began, I gathered with the other athletes in our staging area. While it was a surprise to the American people, we were told President Bush and some of his staff would greet us before the event. Most of us had a chance to meet President George Bush and have our picture taken. It was, of course, the first time that I met the President, or any President. I felt very patriotic and honored that he decided to make an appearance. He wore the blue Olympic leather parade jacket, like the rest of us, and seemed like a regular guy hanging out, telling jokes and having fun. These Olympic Games were so soon after the terrorists attacked on 9/11 that we were all very much aware of the dangerous possibilities. Johnny was especially concerned about the Opening Ceremony. But we felt that we needed to show the world that we were not afraid to assemble in an event where we would be vulnerable to attack. I believe that the President also wanted to send the same message. The people of the U.S. were not going to crawl into their houses and be afraid to live. We wanted to do well for many reasons, and one of those included bringing the world together, even if it was for just for two weeks.

Also with the President was National Security Advisor Condoleezza Rice. I was eager to meet Ms. Rice because I knew she was born in Birmingham. John Zimmerman, Condoleezza, and I took pictures since all of us were representatives of Birmingham and Alabama. John Zimmerman, a Homewood, Alabama, native, had also qualified in pairs skating with his skating partner, Kyoko Ina.

I met several other U.S. athletes as we prepared for the opening ceremonies. We had almost two hours in the gym at the University of Utah as the U.S. team waited our turn to walk into the Olympic stadium. Because ours was the host country, our team was the last one to enter the stadium.

THE PARADE OF ATHLETES

As I walked into the stadium with the other athletes, I could hear the crowd roaring, "USA! USA!" For years, I had watched these ceremonies on television, and now I was one of the people representing my country and walking into the stadium. It was an overwhelming feeling. I tried to find Johnny, but everybody was wearing a white cover, so it was hard to spot him in the midst of the thousands of people.

Marching through the stadium arch and around the track, I had tears of joy running down my cheeks. We waved to the crowd, who roared their approval at our entrance. I kept pinching myself because my childhood dream was actually happening. *I'm here—actually here at the Olympics,* I thought. The impossible felt possible. I knew that, in my own strength, it would be impossible to do what was ahead for Jill and me. Yet because of my faith in Christ, I knew that as I leaned on God for His help and support, all things were possible (Mark 10:27).

Right before we stood and took the Olympic Oath, the spotlight moved around the stadium in a seemingly random way. The spotlight seemed to have no target, but all of the athletes knew who was in the stadium—George W. Bush, the President of the United States. The crowd cheered with excitement as the surprise was revealed and the President welcomed the world to the start of the Winter 2002 Olympic Games. The evening was magical and one that I will recall forever.

Returning to the Olympic Village, Jill and I had quite a waiting game before we could compete in our event. Women's bobsled wasn't scheduled until the second week. Many athletes in other events expressed the same feelings of impatience— everybody was feeding off each other's energy and all of us were ready to compete.

We could only wait until our turn came on the ice. It would be a couple more days until we could get on the ice, so we lifted weights and ran on the university's indoor Astroturf field. Our level of confidence in our abilities was high. The United States' women's bobsled team had two great teams representing our country; either one of us could win a medal on this track.

While Jill and I waited and prepared, we found out that Jean and Gea were having difficulties. Gea tweaked her hamstring in practice during the week before the race, and then reinjured it in a subsequent run. She would find it very difficult to get in shape to give Jean the 100+ percent push she would need for a gold medal. Jean had to consider what she would do if she needed to replace Gea. During that week, Jean called me to make sure that I was set in my position as Jill's brakewoman. I told her I was sticking with Jill. I was confident that Jill was a great driver and I knew she was healthy. If the conditions were right and all of the variables lined up, I knew that Jill and I could win.

THE FAMILY ARRIVES

With hundreds of thousands of people from around the globe descending on Salt Lake City and Park City, Utah, for the Winter Games, hotel rooms were at a premium. I wondered where we could find accommodations for all of my family. Johnny and I turned to our best local friends, Jay and Diane Maynard. For almost two years before the Olympics I had lived off and on with the Maynards while the bobsled team trained and competed in Park City. Throughout the rewards and the disappointments of training and competing, Jay and Diane had been my support system every step of the way. Now we turned to them for help with housing for my family and friends.

Several weeks before the Olympic Games, Diane had broken her leg on a family skiing trip. Because of her forced rest and inability to get around very easily, Diane set up a command post and a chart with the different Flowers and Jeffery family and friends from Birmingham, and began to attack the problem of securing them housing—and also warm clothing.

"Don't worry about the clothing," Diane reassured us. "Just give us a rough idea of their sizes and we'll take care of it." These friends had heard the stories of my own unfamiliarity with the cold weather and the snows of Utah. The Maynards knew these friends would not come prepared for the cold weather of the Olympic Games. Diane tapped into the large community of pilots and family and friends in the Park City area and began to seek extra bedrooms and places for them to sleep, along with finding the clothing. She talked with Jim and Viv Tidd, Ron and Susan Lockhart, Joan and Sven Kristoffersen, Ron and Marcy Allen, Joe and Carol Dalton, Yvette and Harvey Kaplan, and Anita Price, and they ended up housing, feeding, and even clothing several of our family and friends who made it up for the Olympics. The logistics would have been a challenge to most people, but Diane loved sitting in front of her fireplace in the great room of their home and working the puzzle of where to place all of these visitors from Birmingham. After hours of effort, she finally secured a spot for each person to sleep.

When my childhood coach, Dewitt Thomas, found out that I was going to be in the Olympics, he was determined to witness it. Coach, his wife Wanda, his daughter, his son-in-law, and his grandson all crowded in a small car and drove 31 straight hours to get to the Olympics. The Maynards were surprised to learn that Coach and his family were coming to the event—and they had no tickets. Jay and Diane scrambled to get tickets so my longtime friends could get into the bobsled park and have a great view of the event. Coach Thomas had not made a reservation for a hotel in the Salt Lake area because people told him that you could not get a room for less than $200. I was so honored that Coach Thomas would make such a gigantic effort to see the bobsled run firsthand.

While all this scrambling for hotel rooms and clothing was happening back in Park City, Jill and I were in the Olympic Village trying to prepare for the race of our lives. Jill and I had the two beds in our room on either side of the window. We tried to block out some of the light in the window using black trash bags. Nothing seemed to take the edge off our excitement. We tossed and turned waiting for the break of day.

As I had been anticipating being in the Olympics most of my life, Jill had dreamed of the moment throughout her life as well. Since 1994, Jill had been a part of the first group of U.S. women bobsledders. She had trained and had slid around the globe in preparation for this chance to run for the gold medal in the Olympic Games.

For both of us, the night before the race seemed to pass so incredibly slowly. Before any race, you review your various pieces of equipment, like your helmet and your gloves and your shoes. You wonder, *Are my shoes by the door and ready to go and take to the track? Do I have my coverings for the shoes?* Each detail is checked and rechecked to make sure it is all there and perfect. Finally the daylight broke over the horizon and day began to shine.

We headed down to breakfast. Food was readily available in the Olympic Village. But I had to make myself eat, because I didn't have an appetite. I ate a little fruit and cereal and decided that was enough to hold me until later. I knew that Johnny was coming down and I would eat again with him because he was always eager try something new.

I was happy that Johnny was able to ride with us up to the track. The security had been strict about visitors, but they made an exception for him since he had been coaching me as well. The drive up to the track was slower than usual and the miles seemed to get longer and longer, but I knew that this was like no other ride that I had been on. Once we reached the gates, we joked with the security guards as they checked all of our bags and our pockets. They had seen us several times during practice, but they knew this was the real thing. They wished us good luck as we walked through the gates, and encouraged us to win one for the U.S. Several minutes later we emerged from the start house and began our routine. We warmed up and jogged a bit and got our muscles ready for the run of our lives.

THE DREAM
COMES TRUE

Coach Thomas celebrated with me but also had a message for me.
"Vonetta, God did not let you win this medal for you or for me.
The Lord let you win so you can look at another young girl like
you from the ghetto and be able to encourage her."
The message struck me at the time, and I've never forgotten it.

Twelve
THE DREAM COMES TRUE

Waiting is difficult—for anyone and especially for me on February 19, 2002. Jill and I were waiting for our turn to take part in the women's bobsled debut in the 2002 Winter Olympics. It was surreal. I realized that I was the only female African American to compete in these Olympics, but that wasn't my motivation. I knew that there hadn't been an athlete from Alabama, of any ethnicity, to medal in the Winter Olympics, but that's not why I dreamed of standing on top of the podium. I wasn't trying to make history; I just wanted to compete. I grew up in Birmingham, Alabama, and I wished that everyone that I grew up with could see me now. I was a long way from the streets of Bessemer, Alabama, and the corners where I used to roadblock for money to get to track meets. It was cold, the ice was ready, and on this night I wanted to leave my permanent footprints in the snow.

The irony that I had devoted my life as an athlete to track and field and then found my greatest success in bobsled was always in the back of my mind. Yet I had really been following one dream—the dream of being in the Olympics—since my childhood. Sometimes, as adults, our dreams don't turn out exactly like we planned—but in my case, they turned out better. It was a dramatic shift from the Summer Olympics to the Winter Olympics.

Each step of this new direction for my athletic career was

something I knew God had made possible in my life. To some people, it looks like pure insanity to jump into the backseat of a bobsled hurtling down the side of a mountain at speeds over 80 miles per hour. For me, I knew beyond any doubt that God had opened the door for my participation in these Olympic Games.

Each of us on the women's bobsled team had an idea of the significance of what this competition meant for our sport and for other female participants across the globe. Our run this day marked the first time women had competed in the sport of bobsled in the Winter Olympics. The two bobsleds from the U.S. would forever be a part of these historic runs, regardless of the results. As I looked around the start house, my teammates and I were not focused on making history. We were concentrating on the race in front of us and focused on competing at the highest level of excellence. The best women bobsledders from around the were there—including our close competitors from Germany and Switzerland, Sandra Prokoff, Susi Erdmann, and Francoise Burdet, all equally focused on the same goal.

FRIENDS, FAMILY, AND COMMENTATORS
I was extremely happy that my friends and family from Birmingham arrived safely and had a chance to secure warm clothing for the event. They had never been long in this type of weather before. I knew that they would need to be as warm as possible because they were planning to get a good viewing spot at the finish line. Jay and Diane had talked with their friends and they generously arranged to get proper winter clothing for everyone.

While we were at the top of the track, getting ready for the race, my Salt Lake supporters, the Birmingham crew, and Jill's family and friends were very noticeable at the finish line. There were signs that read, "Flowers Power," "Go Jill and Vonetta," and "Go 4 the Gold." Jill's supporters were wearing funny hats, made out of red, white, and blue by Jill's aunt. She even made a few extra hats, which she gave to my family. Some of my family members liked the idea and decided to wear these festive-looking hats. Some had painted their faces and were prepared for the camera if it happened to zoom in on their area. Also, they had created a series of memorized cheers that entertained the growing audience both inside and outside the venue. And every now and then Jill's good friend would let out an eerie sound that was louder and more pronounced than anything I had ever heard, and it would catch everyone's attention. The crowds were huge, mostly new to bobsled, and ready for a good time.

Because a bobsled track is almost a mile long and has a four-story drop in height, each fan watching has to decide where they want to be for the race—either at the top of the track to cheer and watch the start of the run, or at the bottom for the finish line and completion of the race. You pick which part of the run you want to see. Jean and Gea's fans swarmed into the start area of the track while our fans huddled at the finish area. Some fans could view the race on the large TV screens that were set up nearby.

When I watched the television coverage later on video, I found that much of the pre-race commentary focused on the soap-opera-like drama behind the partner switches before the trials. I was not surprised, but I was dismayed at how the situation was portrayed to millions of people. I knew it was damaging to our sport, and that the publicity had turned somewhat negative before the Olympics. It was unfortunate, but none of that mattered at this point. It was made clear that the women had acted the same way men had acted for many years; some thought that women would act differently. Ultimately, every driver made a change in their sled at some time because they wanted to win a medal. It would have been a little easier to digest if it had taken place earlier in the year, but the switching went on for months. The media told part of the story. We were there to give them an ending for the storybooks.

My old partner, Bonny Warner, was in the NBC broadcasting booth. NBC had asked Bonny to cover two events that she knew intimately—luge and bobsled. Bonny brought an interesting perspective to the job; few people had as much technical knowledge of the sport and real respect for the women competitors as she did, but Bonny had also been seriously hurt in the behind-the-scenes drama. I wonder if she was tempted to comment on it all. However, she covered the events professionally and gracefully, and did a great job for the sport she had contributed to so much.

Almost everyone focused their medal expectations on the German and Swiss teams, who were the leaders from the World Cup races a few weeks before in Calgary. The keen observers had followed our training runs and knew that Switzerland's Francoise Burdet clocked the best times. She was expected to go head-to-head with lead German drivers Susi-Lisa Erdmann and Sandra Prokoff. Everyone knew that Jean Racine had the best driving record of any U.S. driver, but since brakewoman Gea Johnson had tweaked her hamstring on a practice run that week, everyone wondered what would happen with them. They were projected as the best medal hopes for the U.S. Jill and I were expected to finish somewhere between fourth and sixth. It wasn't a concern to us whether the fans and the media had expectations for us. We had expectations of our own. We wanted to win!

LET THE GAMES BEGIN

In preparation for the first run, officials sent the forerunners down the track and made sure everything was set for the actual race. The driver for the forerunner sled was former Olympian Pat Brown, the real-life coach of the first Jamaican bobsled team, whose story was told in the movie *Cool Runnings*. Cool! The brakewoman for the forerunner sled was Jen Davidson, Jean Racine's former partner. I watched on the monitor as Jen waved to the crowd and even blew some kisses. Her attitude was terrific considering that just a few weeks earlier she had been training to compete in these Games. It was great to see that she was strong enough to show up and find a way to still be a part of the Olympics. The officials sent down the second forerunner sled with Shauna Rohbock, Jill's former partner, as the brakewoman. She also smiled and waved to the fans.

All of the practices and years of training were about to be measured. It was time to race. There would be two heats. In the first heat, we would race in order, starting with the top-ranked crew from the World Cup season. Jill and I would race tenth. In the second heat, we would race in reverse order, based on our times from the first heat. Switzerland's Francoise Burdet and Katharina Sutter were the first ones down the track. They pushed off at 5.45 and clocked a 49.28 run. Next, Germany's Sandra Prokoff and Ulrike Holzner set a new track record with a 5.33-second start, but had a difficult run and finished in 49.10 seconds.

Now it was time for Jean Racine's USA 1 bobsled team to take the track. Jill and I were inside the start house watching on closed circuit TV when they started their run. Since we went tenth, we were able to look at the other times posted by the top sleds. This gave us an idea of how fast the track was and where we needed to be in order to take the lead. Jean and Gea had a wobbly start and a push time of 5.54, but on the way down the track, Jean drove skillfully and they finished with a respectable 49.31. In the finish area, when Gea climbed out of the sled, it was clear that she had reinjured her hamstring. She was in tears from the pain. Jean had to help her to the truck that would take them back to the top of the track for their second run. Later, the doctors discovered that Gea tore her hamstring to the point that it separated from the bone. Back in the start house, all of the athletes heard about the severity of Gea's injury and knew that it would be impossible for Jean to get a good start time in the next race because of the injury. There are some injuries that allow us to compete even if we're not completely healthy, but having a torn hamstring is like trying to drive on a flat tire. It's possible to move, but the results will be costly if you continue without fixing the problem. Jean knew that she was in trouble.

The next sled down the track was Germany 2 with Susi-Lisa Erdmann and brakewoman Nicole Herschmann. With a start time of 5.39, Germany 2 crossed in 49.19, which put them in the second position behind Germany 1, Sandra Prokoff. Francoise Burdet was in third and USA 1 moved into fourth place.

Jill and I, in USA 2, were the tenth team to compete. At the start area, our coaches picked up our sled and positioned it for the start. They removed any extra moisture on the bobsled, then we placed our slippers inside, pulled the driver's push bar, stood on the block, and lifted our feet to get the ice brushed off. Then we began what had become a ritual for us. Jill and I gave each other a pound. She took her fist and tapped it on top of mine, and then I took my fist and tapped it on top of hers. We looked each other square in the eye and said, "Let's do it." Then it was showtime.

We faced the track ahead of us, focusing and relaxing at the same time. We breathed deeply for a few moments and took our positions at the sled, me at the rear, gripping the push rings, and Jill at the driver's bar.

"Back set," I said.

"Front set. Ready. Go!" Jill said and moved the force of her body to the bar. We hit the sled explosively, at exactly the same time. We had practiced this move until we could do it in our sleep. I dug into the ice with my toes, running towards the end of the start track. I kept pushing as Jill jumped into the sled first, pulled the handle, and snapped the driver's bar into the sled. I felt a quickening in my steps and an extra source of power running through my legs. I think the prayers of everyone from Birmingham to Salt Lake had given me the extra boost that was needed. The start clock told the story—our start time was 5.31 seconds. We set a new start record for the track. We could hear the excited roar from the fans. I'd made hundreds of runs in my bobsledding career, but our Olympic ride felt different from all the others. I remember pushing harder and faster than I had before.

The run itself was perfect. Usually I feel a skid, but this time I didn't even feel a bump. There are 15 turns on the Olympic track, and each time we passed one, I'd think, *Thank God*, because it was so smooth. We didn't make a single mistake and our average speed was 82.3 miles per hour. We crossed the finish line in 48.81 seconds, which set a new track record.

When we crossed the finish line, almost nothing else could be heard but the roaring of the fans around the track. As Jill and I climbed out of our bobsled, our three team coaches dashed over to us screaming that we'd broken the start record just set by the German team. I noticed the applause was also coming from sliders from other countries who had watched our run. We couldn't believe our remarkable time. Our score put us in the lead by three-tenths of a second—which was amazing. In sledding, 0.30 is huge! Jill and I would practically have to crash in the second heat for us to fail. After the first heat ended, I was confident that no one would catch up to us.

We were no longer "the other team." In the break before the second heat, my mom, Bobbie, says that reporters were swarming around her, trying to find out more of my story. She told one sportswriter, "Vonetta didn't see snow for the first time until she was six. She was in track and I always thought she'd be in the Summer Olympics." There were also a growing number of fans cheering for Jill.

Finally, the officials signaled for the forerunners to clear the track for the second heat. Because Jill and I were in the top spot after the first heat, we would go last. Jean and Gea were fifth in the standings as the second heat started. When their time came to compete, I could see the focused and intense look on Jean's face. Gea Johnson was in an immense amount of pain from her hamstring. A few steps into their push, Gea slipped and almost fell. Determined to compete, she limped through the rest of the push with Jean. Their push time was 5.58. Because of Jean's daredevil driving, their times got better as they went down the track. They reached a top speed of 81.7 miles per hour, but despite this, their track time was 49.42 seconds. They had a combined-heat time of 1:38.73. Gea and Jean tearfully waved to the crowd from the finish area, but they knew the United States' hopes for a medal now rested with USA 2.

Switzerland's Francoise Burdet raced next. She had started this competition in the top spot, and after a 5.46 push and a 49.06 track run, she took the lead again with a combined time of 1:38.34.

Germany's Susi Erdmann was next. Her team pushed a start time of 5.39 and clocked a finish of 49.10 seconds for a combined score of 1:38.29—just .05 in front of the Switzerland team.

Next, Germany's Sandra Prokoff made her last run of the competition. Her team promptly beat Jill's and my newly set track start record, with a 5.29 push. After our first run, they knew they would have to break records to beat us. But their finish time was not a track record—48.96 seconds. Their combined score was 1:38.06. When it came to one last team left to go in this second heat, the Germans were in first and second place, and the Swiss in third.

A GOLDEN RIDE

Our sled was the last to compete. For us to take the gold away from the Germans, we had to finish in 49.24 or less. It was going to be critical that we maintain our previous pace for this second heat. As we moved into position in the start area, we were feeling confident. We were ready for the challenge and we knew that for the first time, all eyes were on us. We repeated our handshake and the words, "Let's do it," then we lined up on the sled. We took our deep breaths, focused, and stood in ready position. So many times over the last few weeks, Jill and I had practiced this motion.

"Back set," I yelled.

"Front set. Ready. GO!" Jill responded, and it was like our personal hopes and dreams were combined with the roar from the crowd. We dug our toes into the ice and ran. This single run down the track would be the most important one in our racing careers up to this point. Our push time clocked at 5.33, and as I jumped into the back of the sled and we rounded the first curve, Jill was in her zone and driving perfectly.

Our sled flew around the curves smoothly, one after another. The only thing to mar our perfect second ride was a little bump on curve 14. There Jill caught a glimpse of herself on the large video screen and it momentarily threw off her driving. Otherwise the run was exactly like the first one—perfect. We finished in 48.95 seconds, for a combined time of 1:37.76.

As our sled pulled into the finish area, we could hear the fans chanting, "USA! USA!" and "Bakken, Flowers number one!" As we crossed the finish line on our second run, we held our arms high in the air. I don't remember this; I know it because I saw the photo in the newspaper. I looked up and saw the number 1 by our names. Still sitting in our sled, I was weeping, stunned and unable to move. Jill and I got out of the sled, and suddenly I felt Johnny's arms around me. I could hear him sobbing, his voice overwhelmed with emotion. Then he ran off—to compose himself, I found out later. I ran over to the Bakken-Flowers-Jeffery section and reached across several people to give my mom a quick hug. She looked at me with tears in her eyes and said, "You did it!"

Jill and I hugged and jumped up and down, screaming, "Oh, my God, what have we done?" at the top of our lungs. We hugged anyone we could reach. After several minutes, Jean Racine came to the finish area to congratulate Jill. For many years, this pair had been teammates and raced against each other, and so often in the past Jean had come out on top. Now Jill knew firsthand what it felt like to be the best women's bobsled driver in the world.

After Jill and I went to the media interview area, I was told that I was officially the first black athlete ever to win a Winter Olympic gold medal. Not the first African American, or first black woman—the first male or female athlete of African descent ever to win gold in the Winter Olympics. This news added such significance to my gold medal win. God just added blessing after blessing to my experience that night.

I was thrilled to learn that in the audience for my Olympic bobsled runs was Coach Dewitt Thomas, who had started training me for this when I was nine years old. He, his wife, daughter, son-in-law, and grandson were in the group at the finish line. Coach Thomas celebrated with me but also had a message for me. He said, "Vonetta, God did not let you win this medal for you or for me. The Lord let you win so you can look at another young girl like you from the ghetto and be able to encourage her." The message struck me at the time, and I've never forgotten it.

As many people did, Coach and his family thought the gold medal would be awarded the same evening as the race. Instead, it was awarded the night after the race. This night we would have the flower ceremony. Coach Thomas and his family watched as Jill and I approached the podium where the three top bobsled teams would be recognized. We received our flowers and stood as they played the national anthem. Tears ran down my cheeks. They were tears of joy at what God had done in my life. At the end of the ceremony, to our complete surprise, the two German teams who took silver and bronze carried Jill and me, to the loud approval of the fans. We smiled and tossed our flowers into the audience.

My family and I looked around for Coach Thomas. He had slipped away from the crowd and gotten back in his car. Later I learned that Coach Thomas had to take the Alabama Striders to another track event and he wanted to make sure he was present to handle his team's needs. He missed the gold medal ceremony, but I was glad he was able to watch my gold medal run.

That night turned into a whirlwind of interviews, television appearances, endless congratulations, and getting ready for a 5:00 A.M. appearance on the *Today* show. Jill and I were starving—all we wanted was some food. I had eaten hardly any breakfast that morning. We didn't sleep at all that night because we were going here and there.

WEARING THE GOLD PROUDLY

The next day was the medal ceremony. I wiped the tears from my eyes as we were presented with our gold medals and they were hung around our necks. Ever since I was a little girl I'd dreamed of standing on a medal platform at the Olympics, and now, as it was happening, I was standing on the highest one, and it was almost too much to take in. As they raised the

American flag, I thought of our victory and all that had happened since September 11, and I felt prouder than I'd ever felt in my life. I was so grateful for Johnny and his never-ending encouragement and support. I stood on the podium and proudly sang every word of our national anthem as I placed my hand over my heart. It was a magical moment. Running on ice had provided a way to the Olympic gold that I could have never predicted. I was amazed at how God had honored my simple steps of faith.

Throughout the different public appearances that followed, I often wore my gold medal. Before I won a medal, I had never looked at one very closely. It is distinct from the various medals I earned in track and field (which I continue to prize and value). The Olympic gold medal is about the size of a CD, and each Olympic Games medal has a distinct pattern and design. My medal had the words "Light the Fire Within" inscribed on it. Besides the medal, I received a hexagon-shaped wooden presentation box for it. In addition, the box slips into a leather bag with a drawstring top.

THE JOURNEY CONTINUES

Since I was nine years old, I had dreamed about winning such a medal. Because the 2002 Winter Games in Salt Lake City marked the first time women's bobsled was an Olympic event and because I am the first African American to win a medal in the winter sporting events, the medal is even more precious to me. I feel blessed that my childhood dream became a reality.

After a few months of travel and appearances, Jill returned home, and Johnny and I returned to Birmingham. Even before I got into bobsled, Johnny and I talked about starting a family. About four months after returning from the Olympics, we found that we were going to be doubly blessed, with twins. I had a tough pregnancy and at times I thought I would lose my sons. Fortunately, even though they were premature, I gave birth to twin boys on August 30, 2002. Jaden Michael weighed 3 pounds, 8 ounces, and Jorden Maddox weighed 2 pounds, 9 ounces. Five weeks after the boys were born, I decided to begin my quest for a second gold medal.

I returned to the ice on January 2003 and teamed up with fellow Olympian Jean Racine. We finished sixth at the World Championships in Winterberg, Germany. Jill Bakken took a break from 2002–2004 to recover from a back injury, but as of the printing of this book, she's back in competition again and winning gold medals. Most of our German and Swiss competitors from the 2002 Olympics are still competing. One of our top competitors from the U.S. now is Shauna Rohbock, Jill Bakken's former partner, who decided to become a driver when her time ended as a brakewoman.

As a part of the U.S. women's bobsled team, I am dreaming about the 2006 Winter Games taking place February 10–26, 2006, in Torino, Italy. No one knows what the future holds. Because of my faith in God, I understand the Lord of the universe is ultimately the one who holds my future. I hope that my future includes a gold medal in the 2006 Games. My responsibility is to act each day in faith and work hard toward the goal and see if I reach it again. I'm grateful for the privilege of representing my country in the sport of women's bobsled.

When I answered the ad for bobsled tryouts on a sunny day in Sacramento, California, I had no idea where the journey would take me or that it would bring me to the point of earning a gold medal. You have different goals and different dreams. It's key that you first of all have a dream and listen to your heart. What is your dream? Then make a plan about how you will achieve that dream. You might write it down or you might only do it in your head and never show it to anyone. When you take these simple steps, you've done something important for your life. You've set a goal (a dream) and plotted a course to achieve that dream. Proverbs 16:9 says, "In his heart a man plans his course, but the LORD determines his steps." Ask God to order your steps and plan your course. It will take determination, faith, and discipline to overcome any obstacles that are set in your path on the way to the goal. It's certainly what has happened in my life.

I thought my way to the Olympics would be in track and field through running or jumping in my track shoes. Little did I know that in God's timing, He planned for me to don start shoes with hundreds of spikes, and I would take up the sport of bobsled. It shows the humor and mystery of an eternal God that He can take me from Birmingham, Alabama, and teach me how to run on ice. The adventure of a lifetime is waiting for you. I'm excited about how it will happen for you.

And when it does? I'd love to hear about it. You can reach me through my Web site at www.vonettaflowers.com.

I truly believe anyone can learn to run on ice if they first learn to walk by faith!